AUDACIOUS**NESS**

YOUR JOURNEY TO LIVING
A BOLD AND AUTHENTIC LIFE

**Maribel Ortega
and Helen Strong**

PAPERBACK ISBN: 978-1-7393711-0-4
EBOOK ISBN: 978-1-7393711-1-1

Praise for
AUDACIOUS**NESS**

"What a beautiful book! It speaks to the heart of what so many of us can relate to who have dared to dream and do something different with our lives, to challenge the status quo even whilst struggling with fears and vulnerability."

—Vicky Arundel, Yoga Therapist, England

"Very uplifting and inspiring, particularly all the motivational stories from amazing, strong individuals. The book is really well put together and well written. I got such a positive energy off it."

—Anne Cholawo, Island Adventurer, Scotland

"The best thing about this book is that it's constantly referring to real people who have done real things. It's about LIVED life, not ABOUT life!!"

—Philip Keay, Educator, Author & Spiritual Activist, Thailand

"Very powerful and inspirational! I love the way that you've turned the interviews into a living dialogue between all participants, people who have never met physically. I really enjoyed, and learned a lot from, the trajectories and intersections; 'love' is the big hyphen between all these nourishing worldviews and narratives. Thank you very much for this inspiring work."

—Dr Ousmane Pame, Director of REDES Ecovillages, Senegal

"An enjoyable and inspiring read with so many interwoven examples, painstakingly threaded together into common themes. The questions posed at the end of each chapter are fantastic and provide a great journalling opportunity; it's apt that they are worded both for the already audacious and the wannabe audacious!!"
—Fatema Paretha, Teacher, England

"Fantastic! I loved all the stories and the relatable emotions; I saw myself in many of the people at different times of my life. The questions at the end of each chapter gave me the tools to be honest with myself. I view this book as a guidebook for audacious souls stepping forward with a heart-centered approach. Beware: You may be triggered to create the life you always wanted. AUDACIOUS to me stands for Always Under Divine Authority, Creating Individuality, Often Utterly Soulful!"
—Jacqueline Denis, Writer, Blogger & Poet, Canada

"I love that you cross-reference each guest with their podcast episode in the Appendix – this is genius!!"
—Julie Trager, Writer, Channel & Mentor, USA

"The medicine box needed for our soul in the times we're living in."
—Claire Tonna, Singer/Songwriter, Malta

Contents

Acknowledgements 8

Introduction 10

Helen's story 16

Maribel's story 25

Chapter One: **Triggers** 34

Chapter Two: **Following Our Calling** 43

Chapter Three: **Mindset** 53

Chapter Four: **The Inner Critic** 72

Chapter Five: **Outer Critics** 87

Chapter Six: **Challenges** 101

Chapter Seven: **Role models** 114

Chapter Eight: **Values** 124

Chapter Nine: **Advice** 135

Chapter Ten: **Solid Grounding** 150

A Recipe for Leading an Audacious Life 160

Closing Thoughts 162

Appendix: Our Utterly Audacious Podcast Guests 164

Index of Concepts 175

Further Reading 178

Acknowledgements
Maribel and Helen would like to
offer heartfelt thanks to:

The 41 audacious people who agreed to talk to us and reveal their innermost secrets of what audaciousness means for them. Some of our interviews were quite emotional, many were informative and inspiring, and above all, they were fun! And of course they were the reason that this exciting and extremely fulfilling venture was possible.

The people who stepped up, either by volunteering to come on the podcast themselves, or by recommending other guests that we should interview due to the audacious work they are doing.

The beta readers who gave us valuable feedback on our first draft. The continued support we have received from these people while we have worked on this project has been outstanding and extremely humbling.

Our copyeditor, Denise Cowle, one of the very first guests on our podcast, who gave up a stable and longstanding career in healthcare and now runs a successful copyediting and proofreading business. This book owes a lot to Denise's keen eye and professional work. *https://denisecowleeditorial.com*

Our book designer and typesetter, Amaya Taveras, who first created the podcast artwork and was able, via the image of the little bold fish leaping daringly out of the glass, to effectively communicate our meaning of audaciousness. Amaya is an extraordinary art director and graphic designer. *https://www.amayataveras.com*

Enya Marczak, who at the young age of 15 has shown tremendous professionalism and talent in creating the illustrations used at the beginning of each chapter.

Helen would like to thank Maribel for coming up with the

idea of starting the podcast in the first place, challenging Helen to step out of her comfort zone and put her work 'out there', and providing the much-needed creativity, enthusiasm and support throughout this project.

Maribel thanks Helen for being open to interesting challenges like this AudaciousNess project and giving the scaffolding and organisation that the execution of such plans requires to get results. This structured approach has supported Maribel in stretching her skills beyond what is easy and natural to her, helping her to continue reaching her own potential.

Introduction:
The origin of the *AudaciousNess* podcast and subsequent book

In the summer of 2020, we started meeting online for regular video chats (Maribel was living in Germany at the time and Helen had recently left Germany and moved to Scotland). The topics we were exploring were deep and varied and we found we were enjoying these conversations so much that we felt other people might also benefit from listening in on our discussions.

At the same time, Maribel discovered that some of the women she was coaching were lacking suitable role models, and so we decided to interview 'regular people' who have done bold things in their lives and could, therefore, potentially be role models for others. A podcast seemed the perfect medium for us to get our message out.

Our aim was to showcase individuals who have set themselves bold, audacious goals and have worked to achieve them, with the purpose of inspiring others to act with the courage to create a positive impact in the world. Through interviewing 'regular people' about their audacious goals, we wanted to highlight the fact that role models are everywhere and that each and every one of us can have an impact in some way. Our ultimate goal was to enable a courageous community that honours their genius and lives their calling.

We started interviewing people towards the end of 2020 and launched the podcast in January 2021. Our first guests were either personal friends or people we'd met on social media who had an audacious story to tell.

When we started, we were unsure about how many guests we could find to interview (the self-doubt was already creeping in, which we allude to in this book). So our initial goal for the first year was to record three seasons of six episodes each. However, after publishing our sixth episode we found that we were enjoying the experience so much, and we had guests queuing up to be interviewed, that we kept on publishing without a break and ended the year having spoken with 22 amazingly audacious people.

In 2022, we interviewed a further 19 people, during which time we decided that the podcast had probably run its course and it was time to start collating the experiences and wisdom being shared by these guests into a book.

Where did the name 'AudaciousNess' come from?

The name 'AudaciousNess' came about for two reasons:

Firstly, the 'audacious' part relates to having the audacity to set such a bold goal in the first place. Secondly, we discovered that the word 'ness' is an archaic term for a spit of land which juts out into the sea; in other words, solid ground surrounded by the constant and, at times, tumultuous motion of water. So, for us, Audacious-Ness means having a solid grounding on which to practise your audacity, or, in the words of the great philosopher king Marcus Aurelius (Meditations, 4.49):

> *Be like the promontory against which the waves continually break, but it stands firm and tames the fury of the water around it.*

Interestingly, our understanding of what **audaciousness** actually means evolved as the podcast got under way and we learned other perspectives of the concept. In the beginning, we were using the dictionary definition of the word, which is something along the lines of:

- intrepidly daring
- recklessly bold
- marked by originality and verve
- willing to take risks or do something that shocks people
- doing something with extreme confidence, despite difficulties, risks or the negative attitudes of other people

However, as time went on, we found that we actually preferred alternative definitions suggested by some of our podcast guests, such as this one from Julie Trager:

> *Audaciousness comes about when the pull towards yourself is stronger than the pull towards societal norms. Audaciousness is all about choosing yourself, regardless of how it will be viewed or even regardless of how it will turn out.*

Or this from Dalia Feldheim:

> *Real audaciousness is when we're aligned with our hearts.*

And Claire Tonna actually turned our definition of audaciousness on its head by saying it actually takes more courage to live a *dis*honest life – in which we are *not* aligned with our hearts and are, therefore, doing things that *don't* bring us joy – than it is to be honest and authentic with ourselves. Paradoxically, most of us choose to walk the more difficult, inauthentic path.

So now we're using **audaciousness** to talk about people who have the confidence and willingness to choose themselves and what their hearts are telling them over societal norms. These are people who take risks, not knowing what the outcome will be and despite friends and family not always agreeing with their choices. Audacious people appear on the outside to be bold, daring and sometimes reckless and shocking, although, as we'll learn in these pages, they seldom view themselves as such.

Our reasons for writing this book

We found that not only were we learning so much ourselves from speaking to our guests, we were also getting very positive feedback from some of our listeners. A few months into our venture we knew we were onto something quite significant.

The structure of each podcast episode consisted of us interviewing a guest a few days (or even weeks) in advance, then listening to the conversation again just before publication date and recording our own 15- to 20-minute analysis of what we learned from that guest. Although we occasionally referred to what previous guests had contributed, each episode was independent of the others.

After a while, however, it became clear that we were finding it difficult to keep up with all the amazing journeys being related to us and the invaluable advice being offered. That was when we came up with the idea of summarising our learnings in a book.

This book has three main aims:

- To make sense of what we've learned from the utterly audacious people we interviewed in the last two years.
- To find common threads and patterns from what these people said, and to establish if there is indeed a blueprint or a mindset characteristic of audacious people.
- To offer tips and advice for others who wish to develop their audaciousness, set themselves bold goals, honour their genius and live their calling.

Structure of the book

The book is structured into ten main chapters containing the knowledge and wisdom we've gleaned from interviewing our podcast guests. Our guests come from a variety of backgrounds and we have had the pleasure of speaking with, among others, musicians, coaches, entrepreneurs, teachers, therapists, a lawyer, an IT specialist, a former monk, a business consultant, podcasters, book authors, fathers, mothers and community leaders.

Some of the audacious work these people do could be considered to be for professional reasons, others for personal reasons and yet others for social reasons, with an inevitable overlap between the three domains. When we are doing what we are meant to be doing and living our purpose, this undeniably has an impact not only on ourselves and our career choices but on the wider community around us.

As a prelude to the ten chapters in which we learn from our guests, and to give readers a background as to why Maribel Ortega and Helen Strong, of all people, are writing this book, we present our own audacious stories.

At the end of each of the ten chapters we offer two questions for the reader to consider, based on the concepts presented in that chapter. The first question is directed at readers who **have already done** something audacious, the second at those who **would like to do** something audacious. Whichever group you fit into, we suggest taking the time to jot down your immediate responses to these questions in your personal journal; this will help you reflect on the audacious thing you have already done, or may help you get started on the audacious thing you wish to do.

At the end of the book we offer a suggested recipe for living an audacious life, which is a concoction of some of the key ingredients our 41 guests have used in order to do the audacious things they do. Following that, our closing thoughts give a summary of where we are now and where this journey may continue to take us.

The Appendix contains an alphabetical list of all the utterly audacious people we've interviewed in the past two years. Each entry includes a short summary of the audacious thing that person did, as well as information on how you can access the podcast episode should you wish to listen to the conversation.

The final pages contain an index of concepts presented throughout the book for quick access, plus some suggestions for further reading.

You may find that some of the advice contained in these pages appears to be contradictory. This is to be expected, since collating the opinions of 41 different people at very different stages in their life journeys is naturally going to bring up many different viewpoints.

In addition, the opinions expressed by our guests are only a snapshot of what they were thinking and feeling at the moment we spoke to them in a short (30–45 minutes) interview. There was undoubtedly so much more they could have said, had they had more time, and the opinions and advice they *did* convey may indeed have changed since then, as they have continued to accrue more life experience.

Our advice to readers of this book, therefore, is to take from it what works and resonates for you on the path you are on right now. Perhaps if you were to read this book at a later point in your life, something else will jump out at you or resonate with you. It is intended that this is a book you will return to again and again for inspiration on living an audacious life.

This book has landed with you for a reason. Please know that you are not alone. We are all here to align ourselves with our hearts and do the audacious work the world needs right now. We hope the stories contained in these pages will give you the inspiration to step up and be part of the courageous community of people who honour their genius and live their calling. Are you ready to start this journey? Then let's go!

Helen's Story

U p until the age of 25, my life was pretty conventional. I did everything I was 'supposed' to do according to the norms of the society I happened to have been born into: a small, working-class mining town in the northeast of England. I finished school, got an office job, found a partner, bought a house and stuff to fill it, took annual holidays and tried to be happy. The day I returned from my honeymoon was the day I realised this was not the life I wanted.

With a lack of understanding of what was 'wrong' with me – how dare I not be thankful for everything I had? – I soldiered on for a couple of years, battling depression and feeling desperately guilty for having married such a kind man and therefore ruining his life, such was my state of mind. After all, that's what the women in my family had done before me, and I didn't have any other role models from which to take my cue. However, after two years of living like this, I realised there was no alternative but to overhaul my life on a massive scale.

I left my job, my home and my husband, enrolled at the local university and travelled first to the US and then to Germany, the latter country being one which would feature prominently in my future life. Sometime before, I had felt the urge to start learning German, which I did at evening school before going on to study it as part of my university degree. Responding to this urge was probably the first time I stepped out of convention to follow my intuition and embark upon something without knowing exactly why. In hindsight, I realise this action set me up for what became a well-trodden path of trusting the grand plan and not worrying about the fine details.

I graduated from university at the age of 30 and, still not entirely sure what I wanted to do with my life, at the suggestion of a friend I took a short course in teaching English as a foreign language. This course literally transformed my life when I realised I'd been secretly harbouring a passion for teaching all this time, and I embarked upon a new career path that was to sustain me both mentally and financially for the next 20 years.

With a degree in International Business and German and a certificate in teaching English under my belt, I promptly got a job in Germany teaching business English to employees at a large car manufacturer. I was fortunate enough to be taken on in a contracted position, as most jobs in the profession at that time (and still today) tended to be poorly paid and unreliable. The apparent 'security' of knowing I would be receiving a full-time salary each month made the move to Germany much less hazardous for me than if I'd arrived with no money and few prospects.

I absolutely *loved* my new lifestyle. I threw myself into my work with abandon, absorbing everything I could about teaching English and completing my teaching diploma within two years. My world expanded as I met wonderful people, both fellow teachers and students. My location in the south of Germany meant at weekends I could explore not only the beautiful state of Bavaria but also neighbouring countries such as Austria, Switzerland, Italy and the Czech Republic, and I took every opportunity to learn about my new surroundings.

I took to teaching English like a duck to water. I felt like I'd found my purpose in life. Following my diploma, I did a master's degree and innumerable other courses to learn as much as I could about my new profession. Wishing to share my newfound knowledge with others, I became a teacher trainer, a published author and a conference speaker (boy, did my inner critic have something to say about that one!), as well as a volunteer on the boards of various teaching associations.

After six years on a company payroll I felt it was time to spread my wings and go freelance. In yet another one of my best-ever decisions, I left my second stable job to set up my own business, seek out my own clients and be my own boss. I knew then that I would never go back to working for anyone else again.

A word about money. Shortly after my arrival in Germany I made the prudent decision to buy a small apartment. It was tiny – more of a bedsit than an apartment – and it was to prove to be one of the best financial decisions I've ever made, as we'll find out later in this story. This is not to say that I've always been good with money. If I were to plot my relative levels of monetary wealth throughout my life on a graph, it would look somewhat like a rollercoaster ride, with three main peaks and three main troughs. During the peaks I felt I had more money than I knew what to do with, and during the troughs I sometimes didn't know where my next meal was coming from. This relationship with money – that is, knowing that periods of being broke don't last forever – has helped me develop a level of fearlessness when it comes to my financial situation. In short, I never worry about money.

I'll interrupt the chronological narration at this point to go back to an experience I had in childhood. When I was a young girl

I watched the 1960s American World War II film *The Great Escape*. I remember being entranced by what's probably become one of the most iconic movie scenes ever, where the character played by Steve McQueen is trying to escape from German soldiers on a motorcycle. After being chased across rolling fields in southern Germany in his attempt to reach the Swiss border, the scene culminates in him leaping one barbed wire fence, before being shot at and crashing into a second. I thought the whole sequence and stunts were amazing and so cool, and it triggered a secret desire in me to learn to ride a motorcycle one day.

The opportunity to do that only arose one year after I moved to Germany, when I met Rudi, the man I would later marry. Rudi was a keen motorcyclist and I was eager to learn, so he helped me pass my test and the Alps became our practice ground. This would kick off around 15 years of extensive motorcycling and camping tours covering a large part of Europe, as far north as the North Cape in Norway, south to the Rock of Gibraltar, and west as far as Iceland and the Faroe Islands. Some of these trips were short three- to four-week affairs, but for some we would travel for up to six months at a time.

We loved our motorcycle tours so much that even getting a puppy in 2014 wasn't enough to stop our travels. Spurred on by outspoken critics who said that was the end of our motorbike tours now that we had a dog, we bought a motorcycle with sidecar and some goggles for our canine passenger and set off on a three-month tour of Scotland. We must have looked quite a picture, as people gaped open-jawed and asked if they could take pho-

tos of us. Our story even got picked up by the local press. Where there's a will, there's a way!

A word about Scotland. The country has enchanted me for decades. There's something about the ruggedness of the landscape and the remoteness of the islands tucked away in the northwest corner of Britain that simply captivates me. The culture, the traditions, the music, even the weather – I find it all extremely alluring. I'd been visiting the land north of the border since my early twenties, when my brother moved there for work, and I regularly returned to discover ever more of its nooks and crannies after I moved to Germany.

On one of our earlier motorcycle tours, in 2010, we travelled to the Outer Hebrides, a chain of islands off the northwest coast of Scotland. I remember one very distinct part of this trip when, one sunny day, we came around a sweeping bend in the road and were met with the vista of a whitewashed stone cottage with a thatched roof and a chimney at each end, next to a huge sandy beach and crystal-clear water. My heart skipped a beat and I just knew that I was destined to live in a house like that someday.

On my return to Germany, one of the first things I did was to print out the photo I took of the cottage and hang it on the wall to serve as a constant reminder of my future home. I continued to live my German lifestyle for a further five years, always with the thought in the back of my mind that one day I'd be living in a cottage like the one in the picture – I just didn't know how I would get there.

In 2015, the seed that had been planted in me five years earlier started to sprout and, quite frankly, become quite painful. I could feel it tugging at me. It felt like it was deep in my stomach and that if I didn't do anything about it, it would grow and grow until I burst open. I'd continued to travel to Scotland for holidays each summer, but in 2015 Rudi and I started looking earnestly for my whitewashed stone cottage.

We didn't find one in 2015, nor in 2016, and the ever-expanding seed was starting to get somewhat uncomfortable. In 2017 I flew over to the Outer Hebrides, hired a car and drove around for a few days until I found my beautiful stone cottage with a thatched roof and two chimneys. Or rather, I found a pile of rubble with a collapsed chimney and gaping holes in the roof. In any case, it had 'potential', as the estate agents would say, so I spoke to the farmer on whose land it stood and he agreed to sell it to me.

I flew back to Germany with joy in my heart that I would finally realise my dream, which by then I'd articulated as 'By the time I'm 50 I'll be living in a whitewashed stone cottage with a thatched roof in the Outer Hebrides'.

From a distance, I corresponded with the farmer and the relevant authorities to jump through all the hoops required to restore a ruined cottage to its former glory. I paid handsomely for a flood study report and architects' drawings; I got quotes for laying an access road and I filled in all the necessary forms that the council officers demanded.

In the summer of 2018 I returned to the Outer Hebrides, this time in a campervan with our growing family of two dogs, to oversee the building work on the cottage. It was at this point that I realised this project was going to be a lot more protracted than I'd anticipated. Due to the bureaucracy involved, it quickly became evident that it was going to take months, possibly even years, before approval would be granted and work could be started. I had a decision to make.

I sat down and reassessed my goal, which, in essence, was composed of three parts:

- by the time I'm 50 (when)
- a stone cottage with a thatched roof (what)
- the Outer Hebrides (where)

I asked myself which of these components were essential and

which ones could be modified. I was 48 by this time and I decided that the timescale was non-negotiable. I was becoming increasingly unhappy living in Germany and I desperately wanted to move to the west coast of Scotland. I figured that if I didn't get out before my fiftieth birthday then another year would pass and another, and I just couldn't bear that thought. So I had to act now.

The location was also important to me. Although the whole of the west coast of Scotland is breathtakingly beautiful, and I could have imagined myself living in any number of locations, there was something about the Outer Hebrides that appeared to be calling me.

So that left the building. I decided I would have to give up my dream of living in a whitewashed stone cottage with a thatched roof and two chimneys and look for a 'normal' house. I went to an estate agent, saw a house that I would otherwise have disregarded because it looked so 'ordinary' and asked if I could view it.

The house was situated at the end of a lane, next to a tidal loch (somewhat similar to the fjords in Scandinavian countries) and had been empty for some time after the previous owner had died. As I drove down the single-track road to reach the house, I was overcome with a wonderful feeling of peace. When I stepped into the overgrown garden, even before entering the house, I knew this was the place I'd been looking for.

I mentioned earlier that I'd bought a very small apartment when I first moved to Germany and that this would prove to be one of the best financial decisions I've ever made. Well, in 2017, with house prices in southern Germany skyrocketing, I sold my pocket-sized apartment and with the same money, bought my dream house on a remote Hebridean island. One of the first things my husband and I did after we moved in was to paint it white.

Our primary motive for moving out of the city and into the country was to become self-sufficient in the production of our own food and energy. In addition, since the house we bought was larger than we'd intended, we decided to rent out the spare rooms on a bed-and-breakfast basis, in order to be able to offer others a taste of our idyllic location. Thirdly, I had made the decision a few years earlier that I no longer wanted to support industrial animal farming and exploitation, and so I became vegan. At the time of publishing this book in 2023, I run an eco-friendly vegetarian B&B using locally grown or locally sourced produce with the aim of providing an inspiration to visitors of an alternative way of life than the one we've been societally conditioned to accept. I've discovered that the things I value the most are personal freedom to live how I'm meant to, and living in peace and harmony with nature and with our beautiful planet.

What gives me the solid grounding to continue despite everything that life throws at me is the spiritual journey I've been on for a number of years, which has gained tremendous pace since I moved into my Hebridean home. I trust in the greater plan, I've learned to listen to my intuition and calm my ego, and I know that everything happens for a reason. This gives me such a sense of peace and serenity and fearlessness that I feel equipped to handle any of life's challenges with no limit to my level of audaciousness.

As this book goes to print and I contemplate the next step in my audacious journey, I sense that the primary reason for my co-hosting the AudaciousNess podcast and co-authoring this book may not actually have been to showcase such amazingly audacious people and collate their wisdom and experiences into a guidebook to help other folk wishing to embark on the audacious work the world needs right now. I'm getting the feeling that there was a more important motive for my being called on this venture, and that was to develop the knowledge, skills and expertise as an editor and publisher of podcasts and books in order to be able to assist others in getting their own important messages out to the world and in making their voices heard. To that end, I've already started helping friends achieve their writing and podcasting goals, and who knows where this 'career' direction will lead? What I do know is that, if my actions come from the heart, then I'm on the right path.

If I were asked to offer advice to anyone wishing to pursue an audacious lifestyle, it would be to trust your intuition and do what you feel you are being called to do. Like the seed that was growing in me, if you don't do the thing you're meant to do then that thing you're meant to do will end up destroying you. Once you do what you're being called to do, you realise what your values are and you can then take steps to ensure that the things you do every single day are in alignment with those values. This is what it means to live a truly authentic, audacious life.

Maribel's Story

The day I peed in my pants while watching my parents have a loud fight in front of me was the moment that cracked my self-esteem. That's what I thought for a long time. Many years would have to pass for me to understand the puzzle and put it back together – that it was actually something else.

My parents' separation marks the beginning of my good-girl complex: I say yes most of the time; I'm a stellar high school student; I'm a helpful sister and dutiful daughter; and I almost never stray out of the very well-defined lines drawn for me. If I dare voice an opinion or complain, I am made to feel crippling guilt. I am afraid of confrontation and disharmony, avoiding discussions and differences of opinion. If I come back home too late from a party, I'm a whore. If I gain weight, I'll never be able to 'get' a boyfriend. If I don't have perfect grades, I'm an embarrassing disgrace. In other words, I'm socialised to please others, at the cost of my own well-being or needs.

At 17 I finish high school with the highest grade point average in the whole school and deliver the farewell address at the graduation ceremony in front of parents, students and teachers. I start studying medicine because many family members are doctors, because it's an honourable profession and it's a predictable path, because that would please everyone.

As a young girl I had already fallen in love with literature and writing, most of all with the ability that a story gives you to live and experience someone else's life, and to learn. To dream and escape reality. Later I move from novels to an intense desire to understand human behaviour. Psychology, psychoanalysis, Freud and Jung pique my interest.

I persist for five long years in medical school, but I am a bad student. I am a disaster at memorising long lists of the secondary effects and contraindications of drugs, or all the medical conditions that can cause chest pain. I dramatically flunk therapeutics and physiopathology. Three times each. This causes a minor identity crisis as other than being a good girl and a star student, I don't know who I am.

Getting married at 23 is my solution to that dilemma – to get away from the control, from the stiff, conservative society I am confronted with. We move to South America, where my daughter is born. Switzerland follows and finally Germany.

By this time, I come to realise that I have chosen a tyranny to substitute the one I had before: a dominant personality with almost non-existent empathy, selfish behaviour and extreme preoccupation with their own exaggerated problems. The magical light during these years is my literature studies. Finally, I am able to study what I wanted since my adolescence. I am so passionate about my studies that I can't wait for Christmas and summer breaks to be over and classes to start again.

Some years pass. I've been married for some years and it's a disaster. I feel miserable; I am alone, lacking love and attention.

All I have is my little daughter, with whom I have developed an intense bond. But I have a good life, seen from the outside. I haven't changed much. I'm still the good-natured, people-pleasing person willing to sacrifice her own feelings for the comfort of others. What I don't know is that a tiny seed of contempt had started to grow.

One day I'm sitting alone in the university library, reading. My mind wanders and I break down in tears. I don't like myself; I'm fat and look horrible (or that's what I make myself believe). I am so utterly unfulfilled, and I feel empty and lonely. I ask myself how I can live the next 30 years like this – how will I face my daughter when she's older and tell her that this is okay? I feel so ashamed.

The day I leave my husband, I'm scared like never before. My heart is racing, and I want to crawl into a hole, but I know I need to keep it together for myself and for her. There's no more waiting: this is the moment to take the leap and I can do it. I feel this hint of power, this energy filling up my chest, this confidence that it's possible.

It's a nice evening in late October. I've just turned 31, I have €700 in my bank account and no real job. I don't have a place to live and I'm holding my little girl's hand. We go out into the chilly night to the bus station. While we wait I feel her small hand in mine, I feel the wind touching my cheeks, and I feel this enormous weight rolling off my shoulders: freedom like I've never experienced before, the power that I can make choices. That voice that had been caught in my throat, frozen for so many years, is free and I'm ecstatic. I've no idea how, but I know I can do this. We get on the bus to our new future.

This fresh path brings us to Munich, to a new job and a new relationship with the man I would later marry and who is also the father of my son. Life is good. We do lots of things together – go on vacation to great places, build a beautiful house – and things make sense, life makes sense. I work teaching business English.

I'm not making much money, but that is a minor inconvenience as everything else is ideal.

That is, until my daughter tells me when she is about to turn ten years old that she wants to go and live with her father, and my idyllic life suddenly grinds to a screeching halt. In a nanosecond the vision of my perfect patchwork family falls to pieces. Reimagining a new, different family life is extremely difficult for me, but after many conversations I take what probably is to this day the most difficult decision I've ever had to make.

It's a warm, late August morning the day we pack her things in the car and drive two hours to where her dad lives. She's excited and I'm happy for her. I want her to experience this, but I'm also sad, incredibly so, and afraid of how much I will miss her. I cry alone the whole way back home, wondering if that is what my father felt like the day we left him: a huge emotional black void with daunting chaos and uncertainty.

It takes a couple of years for me to be able to talk about this without tearing up. However, everything I've gone through, even if it seemed insurmountable at the moment, has either had a purpose or taught me an important skill. I remember other parents back then sharing their admiration of me for agreeing with my daughter's decision, but from my perspective (even more so now) it is the right thing to do.

Pragmatism helps me. It makes me focus sooner than later on what I can influence and what I cannot. This mindset helps me focus on myself, let go of control or worry about my daughter when she is not with us, and trust that things will turn out alright.

So I dedicate a great deal of time to myself and my career. I start working more as a corporate teacher of English, doing training, attending conferences and expanding my network. At the beginning of this phase is when I meet Helen. She's first my teacher trainer and later an unofficial mentor as she encourages me to do many new things: volunteering in organisations, writing for a magazine, presenting at an event and more.

The first conference I ever attend is in Stuttgart and it has a couple of hundred participants. I am nervous because I know absolutely no one, apart from Helen of course. On the first day she sees my nervousness and says, 'Hey, relax, do you know how to start a conversation? When you go to a presentation, just turn around to the person sitting next to you and introduce yourself!' I think with incredulity, 'That simple, huh?' Yes, it is that simple!

In the years I work as a business English trainer I discover two things. The first is that working for a language school as a contractor will keep you poor forever. The second is a recurring pattern that I see mostly among women in corporate business: the good-girl complex. I recognise in them a younger version of myself and realise there's something I need to do about it. I feel a pull towards it like it's not me, but something bigger, telling me they need my help. I just don't know yet how I am supposed to tackle it.

In one of the teacher trainings I participate in, coaching falls unexpectedly into my lap. The first time I have a conversation of this profound quality, it's mind-blowing. I can feel how it changes me and helps me shift my mindset. It's a learning and liberating experience at the same time. I feel again that pull from invisible hands and I understand this is something I need to learn. Now I know that this is how listening to my instincts manifests itself to me when it's a positive thing. When it's something negative, something my body is telling me I shouldn't do – that I should say no – it feels like a big rock in my belly.

I decide that the first thing I need to do is stop working for language schools. I have two clients of my own already and after dealing with a huge fear of failure and the feelings of internal chaos that uncertainty brings, I take the leap to put everything into my own business. The second thing is to enrol in a programme to learn how to be a coach. Within a couple of years I transition from language trainer to coach, but this process is not easy. People resist change, and so for a long time I have to decline language teaching jobs until I clearly establish that I only work as a coach and speaker.

I reinvent myself, and with that I learn about personal branding. I also learn about self-esteem and confidence, finding my niche in this space. I think I know a lot about the topic, but I am about to learn a lot more.

Some of the best ideas I have come in a moment of inspiration, without much thinking. Such is the moment when I'm on a call with Helen and I share my frustration that there are not enough female role models for young women. This idea pops into my mind and I exclaim, 'Helen! We should do a podcast about this!' She looks at me with surprise and without much enthusiasm. Luckily Helen recovers quickly, because the next time we speak we start thinking together about this new project.

This is the first time I do something to fulfil myself and I don't care at all what anyone else thinks or how many listeners we have. These profound conversations start a snowball effect of growth in me. It is slow at the beginning, but it increases consistently. During this time I work on a coaching programme that takes me half a year to create and then some more months to improve.

The more people we interview, the more I learn and question my life and choices. I think about the good-girl complex that I supposedly had overcome. I don't know exactly where I am anymore, or where I'm going. It feels as if all my life I have been following rules created by other people, and by the end of the first year of our podcast I am in a dark place without a compass. I am about to find out that the scene of my parents fighting is not what cracked my self-esteem.

After some trial and error, I meet an amazing therapist. She's the one who hands me the compass. A soft-spoken and competent psychologist, she shows me how to finish the puzzle. The biggest realisation of all is that I was raised by a parent with narcissistic tendencies: the constant inability to fulfil expectations; the non-stop criticism about my looks, my clothes, my weight, my hair, my choices; I'm depicted as inferior and imperfect; manipuling my feelings as a teenager, gaslighting any complaints or negative feelings from my side. It all makes sense. And it's brutal.

I spend a couple of weeks crying, mourning the childhood I didn't have. But I'm quite pragmatic, so I dive in. I start to observe how I'm still using coping mechanisms I needed as a young girl with current adult relationships. This is not good. I learn that in some respects I need to finish growing up, spending time on my own and finalising the process of separation and individuation that usually happens in adolescence but narcissistic parents truncate. In other words, create a stronger sense of self and practise autonomy.

This culminates in a five-week summer trip with my son. Every single step in its preparation, every single challenge during this summer, clears more and more of the path that lies before me. I cannot see everything yet, but I have gained reliable trust in the unknown, in the future that is yet to come. I am learning to live a more honest life with myself and speak my truth, because I have the right to, just like anyone else. I now also understand that how other people react to my opinions and needs is their responsibility and choice, not mine. I've shaved guilt off my skin. I've felt enough to last two lifetimes.

I realise that what gives me the solid grounding to continue de-spite everything that life throws at me is pragmatism and trust. I look objectively at situations, assess what I can influence and what

I cannot and then I focus on the former and let go of the latter. Letting go is hard because we have a tendency to want to control outcomes. But what if the outcome of trusting that life will sort itself out is better than you could have imagined? Trusting in a bigger power is not something that I grew up with. I was brought up in an atheist family that sought answers in science. My life has repeatedly shown me, though, that I cannot understand everything, and things that are happening now, even if they are painful, make so much sense later. I'm just at the beginning of this spiritual journey that started with meditation just a few years back. I am practising trust and staying curious about everything I've yet to learn.

I have been seeking in my past the one audacious thing I've done to share with you. I don't have one. Psychologist Nathaniel Branden writes that

> autonomous individuals have grown beyond the need to prove to anyone that they are a good boy or a good girl, just as they have outgrown the need for their spouse or romantic partner also to be their mother or father.[1]

My adult life has been in the pursuit of reaching that autonomy that I was not allowed to create. Now I know where I am. I know what I know and what I do not. I am a work in progress with a lot of potential still to reach and a desire to help others in doing the same. That is an audacious act.

In fact, the whole AudaciousNess journey is part of my work in progress, bringing me space and the desire to explore new things in my life. It has become more than just a podcast or a book; it has become a way of life. As we put the final touches to this book, I'm starting the adventure of living in a new country and have shifted, or, shall I say, expanded, my line of work to amplify the voices and

1 | Branden, Nathaniel. *The Psychology of Romantic Love,* Penguin. Kindle edition. p. 121.

businesses of others from everything that I've learned over the last few years in the areas of personal branding, business and copywriting. I am eager to see and experience what is yet to come.

My advice to someone who wants to be audacious is to be curious and non-judgemental about what they are doing and how they are living their lives, and also to question the reason for living that way. Is it learned and an unspoken expectation of your community, or is it really how you want to live? That will give you the answer of what you need to do. And you need to do it in spite of any fear lurking around. That fear will then go away and that will increase your confidence; it's a positive feedback loop.

Chapter One

Triggers

'She's on her period. That's why she's sitting on the floor.'

This was the response to the question that marketing executive Dalia Feldheim asked on a visit to India, when she wanted to know why a young girl was being served drinks on the floor while everyone else was standing or seated on chairs. Dalia discovered that during menstruation girls in India are considered impure and are banned from entering certain communal areas, including schools. One myth which still abounds is that if menstruating women touch pickles, the pickles will turn sour.

Dalia found this situation humiliating and embarrassing for both the girls and their families, and it triggered her to do something about it. In her position as chief marketing officer for a large corporation selling feminine hygiene products, she created a campaign called 'I Dared to Touch the Pickle' to raise awareness in a humorous manner of these myths that 'don't make sense in the modern day'. Dalia says that of all the marketing campaigns she led in her long career, this is the one she's most proud of.

For many of the people we spoke to, their audacious move was triggered by a specific event. Often this event stirred up such an emotional maelstrom within that it simply couldn't be ignored. Most of the emotions experienced were negative ones, such as shock, anguish, disgust, desperation and frustration. The positive emotions included joy, bliss and love. Whatever the trigger, it was accompanied by a dogged determination to do something about it.

Strong negative emotions that triggered audacious moves

When Jessa de la Morena was diagnosed with cancer, she turned in desperation to others who were going through the same experience. What she discovered, however, was that while people were willing to talk about the grim details of the illness, few were sharing positive and motivational stories to help others on a more psychological and emotional level. This is what triggered Jessa to start the 'U Are the Hero' community.

Jessa told us that she's building the community she would like to have had when she was faced with a disruptive situation in her life and was not able to find the positivity around her to deal with it. She wanted to be able to transform what was happening into something that would give her purpose. So she decided to build something for others, so that

> every single person going through any adversity that shakes the foundations of their life has a place, a community where we can feel not alone, where we feel that others are going through similar things, and where we can read stories that really inspire us and empower us and show us that no matter what that adversity is, there is a way to overcome it and to access that inner hero we all have within.

Jessa wasn't the only one for whom an encounter with a tragic situation led to them embarking on an audacious path. On a visit to his home country of Zimbabwe in 2008, South Africa-based Mark Matamisa discovered that a cholera outbreak there was connected to a lack of access to clean drinking water. Mark says:

> Water is a public good. It's a human right. It should be accessible to anyone and everyone. Failure to have it removes a lot of people's dignity, and it puts societies in very desperate situations.

Although frustrated that this basic need wasn't being provided by the state, at the time Mark didn't know what to do. However, the seed was planted and when a friend later visited the country and returned saying, 'Guys, there's a water problem in Zimbabwe. Could that be something we can tackle?' Mark was driven to action. He and his friends put their savings together and set up an enterprise to provide safe, treated drinking water to a number of families in the country.

In another example of frustration at government inaction, Ousmane Pame, based in Senegal, was driven to action when he realised that the state had basically given up on the task of ensuring people had enough to eat and the country had descended into crisis, with people getting into debt and feeling isolated. Ousmane stepped into the role of educator in his village, first by taking responsibility for a programme that involved visiting neighbouring villages to help with micro-projects, and second by attending a course on eco-village design in India to learn the steps and skills required to turn a bad situation into a positive one. He later became mayor of his village.

It was frustration with the actions of the state and the ensuing indifference to the suffering of others that also led musician and composer Colin O'Donohoe to embark on his audacious path.

Colin told us that the seed was planted in around 2003 with the US invasion of Iraq. He says that at the time, what was being shown on US television was video-game-style footage, showing a little green arrow in the middle and bombs going off. Colin recalls his horror when he realised how this was affecting people:

> I was in a store and I heard a man behind me saying on his cell-phone, 'Hey, man, why don't you come on over later? We'll have a few beers and we'll watch the bombs drop.' And for me, it was quite disgusting that how could we as a people become so far apart, that watching their death and mutilation could be a form of enter-tainment, like a football game, and your buddies come over and cheer it on and swig some beers?

The disgust at this state of affairs led Colin to found an international orchestra comprising performers from all over the world and many different backgrounds. He felt that the best way to bring people together was to remove the perceived distances between them. Colin is aware we're not going to solve racism and political disagreements or change people's behaviours overnight, but through his audacious action he feels it is a symbol that anything is possible.

Denise Cowle's career move was triggered by her anguish at her current situation. She hadn't realised how desperately unhappy her job as a physiotherapist was making her until one evening when she picked her husband up from the airport. As they were driving home he asked how her week had been. Denise takes up the story:

> And on the motorway I just started crying and he was like, 'Okay, something has to change and you're not going back to work until we figure it out.' And I actually phoned in sick the next day and went off with stress.

Denise never went back to her old job and has now found her calling in copyediting and proofreading, running a successful business and even training others in the skills.

Andrea Heuston's anguish quickly turned to ingenuity when she found herself laid off from a leadership position early in her career. Two days later her employer called her and said they'd made a mistake and could she and her team please come back. This was Andrea's response:

> I said I'll call you back. And I hung up the phone and drove down to the state capital and purchased a business licence. And the next day I called the manager and I said, 'Yes, we'll come back. But it will be me that you're paying through my own company.' And then I gave them my business information and they paid me and that's how the company started.

Andrea had decided she never wanted anyone else to control her destiny again. She also decided she wanted to help others achieve the same. More than 20 years on, Andrea's company is still going strong and she's also helping other women, via podcasting and other means, to take control of their professional lives.

It was an incident at work that also changed the course of Angela Papalia's life. She'd been working in a busy law practice in Ontario, Canada, for ten years when something happened that caused her to leave that life and relocate to rural Mexico. She recalls a specific meeting in which she felt brushed aside and that her opinions didn't matter. As she was walking back to her office, she said to herself, 'If this is your life in a year, I'll be very disappointed in you.' This may have set a timeline in motion, because a few months later Angela travelled to Mexico to take part in a yoga retreat and ended up staying there.

American writer and spiritual therapist Julie Trager told us how her life fell apart after she moved to California. Julie had attached so much of her identity to her previous job that without it she felt she no longer had a purpose. She described feeling devastated and bereft, and she turned to God for direction. She recalls praying:

> Okay, God, I don't know what to do. I have no idea where to go. So I'm just gonna lay on the couch and read books for two weeks until you tell me what to do.

During those two weeks, Julie happened to watch a movie about an author and that triggered something in her which set her on a new career path as a writer.

Primary school teacher Nik Pandya, who is working to transform education and equip young children with more relevant life skills for our modern times, told us that the motivation for his work comes from his own school experience, when he felt disillusioned with an education system that rewarded those who conformed and stoked fear in those who thought differently. Nik says he's looking for that 'little Nik' who was held back as a child. He wants to know:

> Who is that little Nik that's sitting there a bit mute, a bit lost, looking at his time when he can play football at lunchtime? And how can I engage that Nik? That's how it started for me.

Entrepreneur Timmy Douglas, whose audacious goal is to alleviate world poverty, was also triggered by events he encountered at a young age. He told us that his world view expanded once he started college and observed homeless people around him. Although Timmy's family had also struggled financially, he realised that what he experienced while growing up was nothing compared to people living without food security and access to water and shelter, and he became determined to do something about it.

Musician and animal rights activist Jen Armstrong made the switch from writing 'mundane' music for the pop industry to raising awareness about the way we treat animals in the industrial farming complex. It was through watching a particular documentary that Jen was triggered to start writing songs through the animals' eyes and become the voice of those trapped in a situation that can be very easily changed, if humans choose to do so.

Kenneth Mackay, who campaigned tirelessly for almost two decades to have a paved road built to his remote island village, was triggered to start his long battle with the authorities when a family member died of a heart attack while walking the only footpath out of the village. That was when Kenneth realised that his community needed a better connection to the outside world in order to be able to summon help quickly when a villager became sick.

Fortunately, not all of our guests had to endure a crisis situation in order to recognise that a significant change was needed in their lives. Some of our guests experienced very positive emotions that triggered their audacious moves, and these were extremely heartwarming to hear.

Strong positive emotions that triggered audacious moves

On a holiday in northwest Scotland in the 1980s, Anne Cholawo noticed a picture of a house in an estate agent's window and was instantly entranced by it. This image was to lead Anne to exchange her hectic urban lifestyle for one of rural isolation on a tiny island without mains electricity, shops or any other modern amenities. Anne explains:

It looked like the sort of house I would have drawn when I was a child. It just threw me and I thought, 'What a lovely house!' And all

> *these thoughts came into my head at that moment. And when I*
> *drove home, I thought nothing would come of it, you know, just a*
> *dream idea. But it just wouldn't go away.*

You'll recall from Helen's story that a similar thing happened to her when she spotted a whitewashed stone cottage with a thatched roof on a visit to the Outer Hebrides in 2010. Although that triggered a vision that she would live in a place like that one day, it took Helen almost ten years to realise her dream. Sometimes the gap between the trigger and the action can be a very long one indeed.

For example, life coach Rebecca Allen relayed a wonderful story that happened when she was a young girl. She witnessed a dog birthing puppies in a very calm and relaxed manner and decided there and then that when she had children of her own she wanted to birth them in a natural and stress-free way. Like Anne and Helen's visions, this one just wouldn't go away. Rebecca told us:

> *Once you've got a vision, you've got some understanding of what*
> *that looks like. I looked up loads of research, I went on a course for*
> *it, I watched videos of women doing different versions of natural*
> *birthing and I thought, 'It's possible. I've seen people do it. It's possi-*
> *ble to do it naturally. I've seen animals do it naturally.' So you get that*
> *thing in your brain that, 'I can do this too. Why not? Why not me?'*

Both of Rebecca's children had natural births, and this was also the case for Maribel. For her there was no research involved; she only felt the pull of her intuition, rebelling against the 'normal' way of birthing in Latin America with anaesthetics and the medical tradition of her family. During lunchtime on a Chilean winter afternoon in Clínica Las Condes, nurses were gossiping about the crazy Dominican young woman who had given birth to a baby girl without drugs. Unheard of!

Interestingly, triggers need not always be at an individual level. Some triggers can affect huge swathes of people at one time. Psychologist Charlene Camilleri Duca, who in 2021 shifted her work online to be able to travel around Europe with her young family, found that the events of 2020, which caused many people in the world to transfer to communicating online, was the trigger which allowed her to realise her dream. Charlene has since observed a shift in mindset among her clients, with people taking the plunge and making changes they wouldn't have done before 2020. Often things happen externally that can have a major impact on the way we live our lives.

This chapter has identified some of those things that have caused people to shift their mindset and impact the lives they live. In the following chapters, we'll continue to follow their stories and learn about what happened to them as they travelled on their new-found paths of discovery towards a new way of living and being.

Questions for the reader to consider

If you **have already done** something audacious, did anything specific trigger the audacious thing you did? If so, what?

If you **would like to do** something audacious, is anything specific triggering the audacious thing you would like to do? If so, describe it.

Chapter Two

Following Our Calling

Whether our guests' audacious moves were triggered by a specific event or not, for many of them something at a very fundamental level appeared to be guiding them towards the thing they were being called to do. Or, as diversity and inclusion consultant Alistair Maigurira expressed it, 'I feel it's a calling for me to be in this line of work.'

'Audaciousness, it's all relative, isn't it?' is what Jen Taylor replied when we said we thought her and her husband's decision – to travel around Europe in a campervan for a year while educating their three kids aged 9, 13 and 15 – was audacious. We found that what one person thinks is a bold move, another may feel is perfectly natural. Jen went on to say, 'We didn't think we were being brave, we just thought we were losing a huge opportunity by not doing it.'

Former Buddhist monk Amaranatho received his calling while visiting a meditation retreat in Australia. He told us, 'I had this strong urge to become a Buddhist monk. And so I did. It wasn't a thinking process. The word "calling" in itself says it just arose. I like to call that clarity.' Amaranatho says that whatever our calling is we simply have to do it, regardless of the impact on ourselves and others, as long as no harm is being done. He quoted a beautiful saying – 'Do what you need to do, otherwise the thing that you need to do will kill you' – and explained that if we each do what we need to do, ultimately, on a collaborative, collective scale, change will happen.

In other words, if we all do what we're meant to be doing, the world will be a better place. By ignoring our calling, the thing we're meant to be doing will eat us up from the inside in its urge to get out and we will, in effect, be contributing to keeping the world in a 'stuck' place.

Anne Cholawo expressed similar sentiments to Amaranatho. Although Anne experienced a specific trigger (seeing a photo of a house on a remote Scottish island, as mentioned in Chapter One), she explained how she then responded to a strong urge to do what she was being called to do, despite not knowing how it would turn out. She told us that ever since she was a child she'd dreamt about living in the middle of nowhere, and when she saw the house she couldn't stop thinking about it. She recalls, 'I remember being on the boat going home, looking back at this house getting smaller and smaller and thinking, "I can't leave this place. I want to be here."'

As soon as Anne returned to her home in the south of England, she sold her property, gave up her job and made an offer for the house on the island. Within a matter of months she'd moved into her new home, 'where there was no electricity, no ferry service and I had no idea how I was going to make a living. The whole thing was, at the time, terrifying. But at the same time, I had to do it.'

So, how do we recognise when we are being called? We come into this world with unique talents, interests and abilities. Unfortunately, modern society tries its best to dull our individuality and uniqueness in its quest to homogenise us, since the industrial system, based on maximum profit for the few at the expense of the many, needs unquestioning workers who are ignorant of their own power and potential. Fortunately, there are many audacious people who are willing to step out of this level of conditioning, recognising their own value and responding to the impulse that is calling them, thereby showing others what is possible. Colin O'Donohoe is one of those people.

Colin is an outstanding composer, musician and arts advocate who founded the Pangean Orchestra, an ensemble of performers and instruments from all over the world. Colin was fortunate enough to have recognised his own talents and interests at a very young age, knowing since he was just five years old that he wanted to be a musician. He told us:

> Nothing makes me feel as alive as when I'm composing or performing music. When I wake up in the morning, I have this unbelievable passion and self-belief that I can do it. I can be happy with my life if it was to end today.

Colin spoke of an excitement about what he does and is sure he will have the same level of excitement at the age of 80, or even 100!

Another musician we spoke to, Maltese singer/songwriter Claire Tonna, shared a similar view. Claire writes because of an impulse to hear things that give her peace in a world filled with injustice and unbearable human emotions, such as loss, grief, rejection and abandonment. She told us that from a very young age she's been writing things that give her strength and faith, no matter what happens in the world. This led first to Claire composing her own songs, and second to discovering that she had been gifted a voice to sing them with. Claire says, 'I write what I need to hear and I sing the words that give me strength and courage.'

Maryam Mohiuddin Ahmed, who has dedicated her life to social justice and human rights, was also able to recognise her calling at a young age. Maryam told us that ever since she was a child she has had 'a sheer fervour for social justice'. This led to her studying human rights in law school and then setting up the first social enterprise incubator in her home country of Pakistan. Maryam discovered her calling by recognising what was going on for her personally and what gives her life and hope. However, she said that actually *following* her calling was a more difficult decision to make and 'something I was constantly questioned for. But, eventually, it became something that I'm constantly rewarded for.'

Marketing executive Dalia Feldheim discovered early on in life that her purpose was to empower people, especially women, to be the best they can be. Dalia told us that 'everything that happens to us in our life, all our highs and our lows, determines what our purpose is', and once we've established that, we need to ask, 'How do I bring my strength and passion areas into what the world needs?' Dalia was able to use her position in a large multinational corporation to bring forth her strength and passion and make a meaningful impact by creating an award-winning marketing campaign, which went on to become an icon for women's empowerment in the world.

Our youngest guest on the podcast, Katie Taylor, who was only 18 when we spoke with her, already knows what is calling her. Katie's audacious goal is to become an expert in natural horsemanship, a practice of building close relationships with the animals and letting them be your teacher, somewhat akin to being a horse whisperer. Katie says she's always had a love for horses and she also recognised at a very young age that relationships (with both animals *and* humans) are important to her. Natural horsemanship, therefore, seemed the natural path for Katie to take.

Sometimes it takes a little longer for us to recognise our innate talents and strengths, and we may follow seemingly unconnected paths on the way to developing the skills and abilities required for our ultimate calling.

Debbie Levitt was always interested in technology, referring to herself as a 'computer geek' growing up. However, she later discovered she also had an interest in human psychology and ended up combining that with her skills and talents in computers to set herself the audacious goal of fixing problems in the user experience (UX) industry. In the 1990s, as the internet was taking off, Debbie felt the urge to learn how to make webpages, recognising that her skills and talents in this area would be critical for this new technology. She realised that people would be willing to pay others to create websites, but she recalls thinking she 'didn't just want to throw pages together' and that she wanted to incorporate the psychology concepts she'd learned into her work. She admits that, although she hadn't heard of UX at the time, ultimately that's what her line of work was all about.

Farhana Yamin told us she was always interested in working for social justice, having done voluntary work to help immigrants and other people with housing and employment problems. After studying to become a lawyer and therefore 'conforming to the expectations of academic achievement within Asian societies and the status and prestige that goes with that', Farhana chose to specialise in environmental law, and began a career which has seen her campaigning for worldwide environmental justice for over 30 years.

There's no doubt about it, it takes guts to step away from societal expectations, to stand up and say 'no, I'm being called to do something else'. But if our path is not entirely clear to us, how do we go about finding out exactly what it is we are being called to do? The key is stilling the mind, going inward and feeling what is right. Myah Payel Mitra, who left a corporate city job to set up her own business as a movement therapy practitioner and career transition coach, describes this as living life by design, not by default. To do this she went on an inward and reflective journey, searching internally for meaning, and emerging with the realisation that her purpose is 'to help others through my words, through my work and through my life'.

Similarly, it took Maribel a long time to put together the pieces of what her calling was. As an adolescent living with a parent with narcissistic tendencies, she learned to read unspoken cues of gestures and body language to predict what a reaction would be. This coping mechanism of hyper-empathy and other-centredness would later become her superpower in coaching people. Maybe her inability to understand why she was never enough was what made her interested in human behaviour and, later, coaching. The final piece was seeing herself in the young insecure women she was working with. When Maribel is coaching someone to discover how to assert themself, time stops and nothing else matters. She's in pure blissful flow.

Seeking the services of a life coach is indeed one way to discover what our calling is. Entrepreneur and life coach Timmy Douglas told us he loves helping people achieve their dreams and goals. He wants to motivate people to be authentic to themselves, and so he started a podcast to reach more people. In talking about his podcast, Timmy explained, 'It's what I love to do. I would do it for free for the rest of my life. I will always talk to people about their dreams and goals.'

Motivational speaker Gavin Scott says that 'we all have a purpose and that purpose needs to be passion-driven'. He warns about following a goal without awakening to a higher level of consciousness, otherwise we'll just end up robotically going through the motions. Like Myah, Gavin has looked within himself and found that trying to change habits, create a better environment and serve people to fulfil their true potential aligns with what is calling him.

Another life coach we spoke to, Rebecca Allen, made a similar discovery about what was calling her. Rebecca was working in the advertising industry and her corporate job was 'driving her nuts', so she followed her calling to set up her own business as a coach. She recalls 'sitting many times on the same park bench at lunchtime, trying to work out what I wanted to do with myself', finally reaching the conclusion that she needed to focus on her strengths, passion and energy. Since she'd been doing a lot of work on her own personal development, it seemed a natural step for her to offer to help other people wishing to develop themselves. This is how Rebecca describes her work now, and why she does it:

> It's an amazing experience helping other people become their true power, their true authentic selves and having that presence they really want to have. That's a life-changing skill to learn. And that, for me, is massively gratifying and it's why I do what I do.

Massively gratifying indeed! Once things fall into alignment and we are following our calling and honouring our individual strengths and passions, it's *extremely* rewarding and gratifying. We asked Denise Cowle, who left her physiotherapy job to become a freelance editor and proofreader, whether she felt she had found her passion now. She admitted, rather sheepishly:

> I do, actually, which is such a nerdy thing to say about editing and proofreading, but I do love working with words and language. I really get such a lot of pleasure out of it.

Not only does Denise get pleasure from her own work, but

she's also actively encouraging new editors and proofreaders into the profession, first because she loves connecting with other people, and second because she wants the industry to flourish and grow. She calls this paying back the friendly welcome she received from her peers when she first made the transition into her new career. As Amaranatho mentioned at the beginning of this chapter, if we each do what we need to do, ultimately, on a collaborative, collective scale, change will happen.

Julie Trager was also working in healthcare (or 'disease management' as she prefers to label the current healthcare model) when she decided to make the transition into alternative medicines and natural remedies after developing an illness for which her doctor prescribed medication for the rest of her life. Julie told us she refused to accept this diagnosis and so started doing her own research about her illness, realising that not only was she burned out from her current career, but that there was a whole new world of medicine out there that she hadn't known existed. Julie started working to heal her body through more natural means, such as diet, supplements and meditation, and found she didn't want to be part of the conventional healthcare system any longer. She quit her job, got certified and started a health coaching business.

In a similarly bold career switch, yoga therapist Vicky Arundel spent many years working for a computer gaming company before she returned to the passion she had discovered when she was only 15. She spoke about it being a 'foregone conclusion' that she would end up in this line of work. Vicky told us:

Yoga has been part of my life for such a long time that maybe it was an obvious foregone conclusion that I would end up in this place.

It was perhaps also a foregone conclusion that Thailand-based educator Philip Keay would find his calling in travelling and teaching. Philip told us that when he's either travelling or teaching he's absolutely in the moment, loving just being there, connecting with positive people and simply feeling 'it's a joy to be alive'. Philip 'accidentally' emigrated to Thailand but is aware that things don't happen by accident, and that if we approach life with an open mind and an open heart then whatever is calling us will present itself without us actually planning for it. We need to trust the greater plan and go with whatever it is we are being called to do or be.

Primary school teacher Nik Pandya also realised his passion for teaching, telling us that when he embarked on his new project of teaching children 21st-century skills he would lose track of time, get lost in his research and talk very passionately about the topic. He said:

> I was very enthusiastic about it. It never got old. It never got boring. And I was always thinking, 'I need to improve. I need to learn more. What more can I do?'

Singer/songwriter and animal and human rights activist Jen Armstrong is now living her passion of being a voice for the pain and suffering of abused and oppressed people and animals. Jen told us that her songwriting has transformed from composing 'meaningless pop songs' to now living an authentic life and being who she wants to be, singing about things she cares deeply for. In recalling her previous songwriting work, Jen asked herself, 'How can you put passion across to your audience when you're not feeling it yourself?'

How else can we recognise when we are being called? Perhaps we inherit our passions from our parents or from previous generations. For example, professional housesitter and digital nomad Susanne Hillmer talked about having a nomadic gene in her blood, and marathon runner Tish Joyce said her late father was also a runner.

Or could it be that destiny is the deciding factor in what we are being called to do? When Scottish islander Kenneth Mackay was offered an easy life running a fruit farm in Australia he refused, as he felt destined to stay in the place he grew up. As it turned out, Kenneth proved to be instrumental in getting a road built into his village to stop it being abandoned and to save the villagers from evacuation.

Whatever we are being called to do, it is imperative that we then take action to bring our dreams into fruition. To do this, audacious people have developed a certain mindset which allows them to continue with their purpose, no matter what life is throwing at them. Let's turn now to what our guests shared about developing this audacious mindset.

Questions for the reader to consider

If you **have already done** something audacious, did you feel a calling to do the audacious thing you did? What did it feel like? Where did you feel it in your body?

If you **would like to do** something audacious, do you feel a calling to do the audacious thing you want to do? What does it feel like? Where do you feel it in your body?

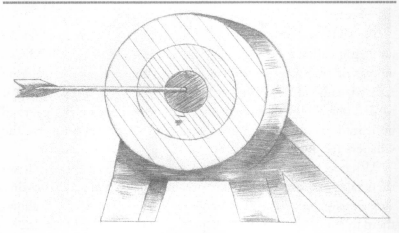

Chapter Three

Mindset

During and after all the conversations we had with our guests, we were interested in finding out the commonalities that came up again and again in their behaviours and attitudes. It was for us a sort of investigation, or diagnosis if you will, of what attitudes these intrepidly daring people share and whether this is something that can be learned by those who decide to live their lives in a more audacious way.

We discovered eight main approaches that build the basis for living an audacious life:

1. Set goals
2. Make plans
3. Let go of control
4. Know your worth
5. Abandon the victim mentality
6. Think like an entrepreneur
7. Have faith and trust
8. Believe you can do it

1. Set goals

In the introductory chapters, Helen explained how, at the age of 48, she set herself the following goal: by the time I'm 50 I'll be living in a whitewashed stone cottage with a thatched roof in the Outer Hebrides. That's a pretty specific goal, and you'll recall she managed to achieve two of the three specifications, which is not bad! But, in general, do we really set ourselves such specific goals? And if not, why not?

One reason we don't set goals is that our education systems fail to teach us how to in the first place, never mind how to develop plans to achieve them. Modern society wants workers who follow orders, not entrepreneurs who can think for themselves. The first step on the audacious path is to find out what it is we want to achieve and how we want to live our life. Or at least find out what it is we do *not* want.

This is what IT executive-turned-coach Myah Payel Mitra did. Myah told us that on her deathbed she didn't want to regret having lacked the courage to live her dreams, so she spent some time clarifying what it was she wanted. She told us:

> *I wrote myself big, hairy, audacious goals. I knew that I was ready to start a new chapter of my life: not only a new chapter, but a new book.*

As it turned out, that new book meant leaving behind a comfortable corporate life and tapping into unknown new territory. As Myah beautifully put it, 'When you are on purpose, even if you fail, you will fail on purpose.'

Failing to explore that unknown creates what musician and composer Colin O'Donohoe calls 'stillborn ideas'. Colin believes 'everyone has a budding audacity somewhere, but those ideas need resuscitation'. So we need to take those ideas and give them more form, creating a clear vision of what it is we want. As entrepreneur

Felicia Specht puts it, 'The more defined your dream is, the easier it is to set your obstacles aside and to follow your dream.'

This is also how Denise Cowle decided to approach her situation when she made the career switch from physiotherapist to copyeditor. Denise told us she was 50% excited and 50% terrified, but once the decision was made it became easier. She had made up her mind that, regardless of the outcome, she would not return to her old job. Denise said:

> It had reached a point where I thought, 'I have to do this, I have to at least try.' The overriding feeling was, 'If I don't get out and try something now, I'm never going to do it.'

Denise's mindset of getting out and trying something new and therefore viewing life as a continuous learning process, is one also shared by Lynn Yap. Lynn's career has taken her from law to investment banking to launching a network supporting women and girls in work, to authoring a book. Lynn constantly pushes herself outside her comfort zone 'to continue to be curious, to not be afraid to learn new things and to never be too old to learn new things'. For Lynn, constant learning and achieving her goals is part of being alive.

One thing that's important when setting our goals is to aim for balance in our expectations – not too high that we don't reach them and then become disappointed, but not too low that we avoid achieving our full potential. Rika Cossey, who set herself the audacious goal of attempting to live as self-sufficiently as possible, thinks we are bound to fail if our expectations are too high. On the other hand, if we have none we'll never be positively surprised if we exceed those expectations. Rika explains that the sweet spot is a balance between the two extremes. If something doesn't work for her then she constantly evaluates her goal and tries something else.

It must be emphasised that creating the outcomes we desire

is the responsibility of each and every one of us. No one else can possibly have the same insight into what our personal goals are as we do ourselves. Life coach Rebecca Allen firmly believes that what we choose to do and what we choose *not* to do is well within our control, and that it is possible to achieve excellent outcomes and create our own luck if we only set goals and work hard at achieving them.

Interestingly, as a counterargument to the above, we spoke with Philip Keay, who told us how he 'accidentally' emigrated to Thailand, where he 'accidentally' became a teacher. Philip explains the accidental quality of his life like this:

> If I'm open then that means things will happen in my life that I hadn't planned. And I didn't really plan anything, so I suppose the accidents happen because I approach life with an open mind and an open heart.

More than 30 years later, Philip is still loving life in the place he didn't 'plan' to be!

2. Make plans

Having said that, we do believe goals are important, and once we've set our goals we need to start making plans to achieve them. Business consultant Mike Patterson told us that when we fail to plan, we're effectively planning to fail, a concept he terms 'default theory'. Goals without plans are just pipe dreams and we will end up resorting to the default, which is not to achieve what we want. For example: if we don't have a health plan, we're planning to be sick; without a wealth plan, we're planning to be poor; failing to have clear expectations in our relationships means we're planning to have disagreements and conflicts. Planning brings clarity into our lives.

Podcaster Timmy Douglas expands on Mike's 'default theory', in particular the wealth plan. Timmy gave us the example of some- one born into a poor environment, surrounding themselves with other poor people of similar mindset and having a hard time get- ting inspiration or ideas for breaking out of the pattern of pov- erty. Timmy says the easiest response to such a situation is 'I'm destined to be broke because nothing is working in my favour'. That's default theory in practice. Timmy encourages us to plan, take action and get the information required to move ourselves into the place we want to be.

Motivational speaker Terry Tucker says a major problem is that people live a casual life, and as a result their goals, dreams and am- bitions become a casualty of that unplanned living. Indeed, ideas and visions without a goal or plan are simply dreams that nev- er materialise. Without goals and plans we are setting ourselves up for failure and the personal disappointment of never reaching those things we so desire.

3. Let go of control

Our human brains are like small prediction machines. They would love to know how everything in our lives will develop. Our brains love habits and routines because then things are predictable, which is much more economical for the brain from the perspective of resources and energy consumption. When we learn new things, or when we don't know the outcome of something, it requires more concentration, more energy and more resources in general. This is where the innate desire to control comes from. At the same time, our brain is a fantastic organ that can adapt and learn at any age, for as long as we live. This is what is known as neuroplasticity.[1]

Trying to have control over everything will not serve us in the

1 | Rock, David. *Your Brain at Work*. HarperCollins, 2009

long run. We need to focus on what is within our control and accept what is not. We need to accept that not everything will be 'perfect' (assuming this state even exists). If we stay mindful and in the moment, this will help us realise what is in our control and what isn't. Maribel mentions letting go of control as a common thread in her life's story, particularly when her young daughter made the decision to live with her father.

Even when the 'worst' happens, if there's nothing we can control we simply have to accept it. Award-winning entrepreneur and CEO Andrea Heuston relayed the tragic story of witnessing her home burning down after a chimney fire hit the cedar roof and the house went up in flames. She recalls standing across the street watching the inferno – a situation over which she had zero control – and asking herself what she could do about it. It was then that she realised there was nothing to do except be in the moment. With the benefit of hindsight, Andrea told us:

> I truly believe that, when I get a little cocky, the universe says, 'No, don't do that. Here's the lesson you must learn.'

Thankfully, the universe has provided nature to teach us how to let go of control. Maltese singer/songwriter Claire Tonna shared a beautiful image with us. She said:

> If a little seed tries to think logistically how she's going to become a tree, she's going to have a breakdown. She's going to say, 'This is impossible.'

But this is precisely what *we* do, trying to control how we are going to get somewhere. Claire believes that everything that happens in our lives is helping us arrive at wherever we need to be, and it's natural that we'll go through periods of darkness. We need to learn to trust those 'out of control' patches. This is what Claire calls completeness.

Life coach Rebecca Allen has learned to be okay with the fact that she cannot control everything and sees that as part of the journey and learning experience of life. She believes that when we have a knockback we need to adapt our expectations, since sticking rigidly to the original plan will just create disappointment. Like Andrea, Rebecca says we need to focus on what is in our control, for example:

> Who you decide to be in a relationship with is in your control, how they behave towards you is partly in your control, but you have to draw the line as to where your control stops and their control starts.

Control, or lack of it, is an important factor when obstacles appear. They are part of the path and are there to test us, and we need to be flexible and ready to adapt to them when they show up. Alpha-Vitamin woman Aurora Pérez-Vico told us she used to panic when things were out of her control. Now she is learning to adapt to unexpected situations that arise. For someone who describes herself as a control freak, Aurora is proud of the fact that she's managing to overcome this.

A strategy employed by copyeditor Denise Cowle is to ask herself 'what's the worst that can happen? And if that thing were to happen, what then?' It's good practice to follow this line of thinking through, i.e. to continue the process of asking ourselves what would happen then, and then what, and then what else?

However, Thailand-based 'accidental' teacher Philip Keay makes an important distinction between external control and self-control. We may not be able to control what happens *around* us, but we certainly can – and most definitely should – control what is happening *within* us. Philip warns that 'if you don't have self-control, you will spend your life trying to control other people and other people will be controlling you'. Becoming very clear on the things we have control over and the things we don't gives us freedom and power and allows us to pursue our audacious goals with much greater ease.

4. Know your worth

We are worthy and deserving of what we wish to achieve, and one way of countering any doubts we may have about this belief is to build up a body of evidence to support it. Life coach Rebecca Allen recommends repeating the mantra 'I deserve this and I am worthy of this' and then to think objectively about what it is that makes that true. For example, it could be something like 'because what I'm saying is interesting, because I've got this background, because I've got this education, because I've got this passion in this area'.

Similarly, Andrea Heuston advises us to 'always come into the room knowing that you deserve a seat at the table and you are just as worthy of being there as everyone else'. If we are an expert in our field, then we are providing a service that others need and that they cannot do on their own. Specifically addressing women, Andrea adds, 'We are just as worthy of being there as anyone else. And if you don't believe that, you're not.'

Singer/songwriter and animal rights activist Jen Armstrong spent much of her career writing 'meaningless pop songs' before she realised she was worth more than that. Although she knew writing and recording songs about what she really believes in would not be as 'lucrative' as her previous work, Jen nevertheless shifted her focus to bringing her passion and worth to the table and to the world.

Likewise, tech expert Debbie Levitt knows she is making a worthy contribution to the world with her work, her advice and her techniques. Debbie's reward is simply the knowledge that she is creating positive change.

Motivational speaker Terry Tucker says we are all born uncommon and extraordinary, regardless of our job, where we live, how much money we make or what car we drive. Although we're not all born with the *same* gifts and talents, we all possess the ability to become the best person we're capable of becoming. Terry says our gifts and talents are unique to each and every one of us and we should search with an open heart for our purpose in life. Then we'll know our worth.

Having this knowledge of our worth is extremely grounding, and when we start believing we are worthy then we are in an audacious mindset. At any given moment we are exactly where we are meant to be in our lives, yet there is always something new to learn. We must remember that we are a crucial part of the whole and we all have a worthy contribution to make. We need to value that.

5. Abandon the victim mentality

Things happen randomly, without any seemingly particular reason. They are neither good nor bad, they just are. However, how we choose to respond to them makes all the difference. We need to avoid slipping into victim mode and instead keep a positive mindset and ask ourselves, how can I make this situation work for me? The trick is to reframe what is happening to us in a more positive light that helps us see the learning potential or improvement in our lives. In other words, we can view adversity as a gift.

Jessa de la Morena is one fantastic example of having been dealt a particularly bad hand and flipping that in a way that empowered her. Jessa battled cancer twice, and through that discovered her inner hero. She asked herself, 'What if the worst thing that ever happened to you was the best thing that could have ever happened to you?' Jessa was living an intense, fast-paced life with kids and a full-time job, and no room left for questioning whether the life she was living was aligned with her essence and her values. Jessa views her illness as a gift, saying, 'The gift that cancer gave me was it stopped me in my tracks.'

Jessa's condition forced her to halt and process many difficult emotions that catapulted her into a journey of introspection. For a long while she didn't know what the outcome would be, and when forced into this extreme situation two things became very important to her. One was to make the most of every single moment, despite going through tough medical treatment, and the other was the realisation that she had a completely white, brandnew canvas that she could choose to paint however she wanted. This caused Jessa to start thinking about what she wanted to do and what that perfect situation would be like for her, and then taking steps to make that happen.

Jessa decided to take a positive approach to her future and look within, trusting herself. She mentions how we've been programmed all our lives to look outward from ourselves, that someone else is the 'expert' who can save us, and that we need to unlearn and break free from that and 'realise the actual hero resides within'.

Motivational speaker Terry Tucker explains that what most people tend to do when they encounter a challenge or impediment is to blame something or someone else. He told us, 'Very few people take personal responsibility for their own success and happiness.' Although Terry has also battled cancer, he doesn't blame anyone or anything for his illness, believing that 'God has given me the strength to get through some pretty dire and dark times'.

Of course Terry has days when he feels sorry for himself, but he's found a method to help him move forward: he starts looking outward. That helps him focus on another human being rather than himself. He finds someone for whom he can make a difference in their life. It could be as simple as just asking how they are or if they want to talk and have a cup of coffee. He says that although cancer can affect all his physical faculties, it cannot touch his mind, his heart or his soul. And that is who he really is. Our bodies are just a vessel to house who we really are. He encourages us to 'spend more time worrying about and developing who you really are and less time about how you look and what kind of clothes you're wearing and stuff like that'.

Entrepreneur Andrea Heuston has a particularly interesting and clear approach to not playing the victim. Andrea's conviction is that 'things don't happen *to* us, rather things happen and we choose our reaction to them'. Choosing to take responsibility is key, as is knowing what you're *not* responsible for. Andrea's remedy is 'choosing your reaction to what happens in life, moving forward and learning from it'.

Maltese singer/songwriter Claire Tonna views life as an ecosystem in which everything that is happening around her is part *of* her and conspiring in her favour, even if at that moment she can't understand it and would rather it hadn't happened. Claire practises trust, in both life and in herself. This means as soon as something unexpected and unwanted happens, she convinces herself it's going to be alright as this is what needs to happen right now.

Another way that we can put ourselves into victim mode is when we burden ourselves with other people's problems. We think we are helping to shoulder the load but, in fact, we are doing neither ourselves nor others any favours by behaving this way. We need to mark our boundaries and reinforce the fact that we are each responsible for our own lives.

One way we can do that is simply to say no. This is the strategy lawyer Angela Papalia adopted after deciding to move to Mexico from her native Canada, leaving many friends behind. To focus on her new life Angela needed to set boundaries in the old one, and she found she became very good at being able to say no. She discovered that 'no, I'm not doing that, I don't want to, I don't feel like it, I'm not in the mood right now' are, in fact, good enough answers. Angela proudly recalled an incident where one of her friends reached out to her and she felt able to respond without guilt:

> I can't be that person for you right now. I can't relate whatsoever to what you're saying. I'm your friend, you'll always be my friend, I'll support you. But I can't be that person that you need right now. You have a whole great circle, a husband and friends. I'm sorry, you're gonna have to ask one of them.

Angela has learned that saying no allows her to work much more efficiently and effectively, since not getting caught up in other people's problems enables her to stay more focused.

Charlene Camilleri Duca has first-hand experience of people in victim mode through her work as a clinical psychologist. Charlene says, typically, people stand in their own way by limiting themselves or their opportunities. They express desires like changing careers, travelling or having a particular type of relationship, but then harbour the belief they can't have it. Charlene says, 'The only thing that stands in their way is their limitations – what they think they can do or what they feel they can achieve.'

When we take responsibility for that first step, we realise it's only our fears that are creating limitations. But those fears are not real – they exist only in our heads. Charlene says the trick is to shift from the mentality of 'I can't, this isn't possible' to 'Why can't I? What's stopping me? Who's stopping me? What's so difficult about this?' When we do this, we realise that, even if no one we know has set themselves this goal before, it may not be completely outrageous. When it ceases to be a big deal, who knows where it can take us?

Being able to say no unapologetically and take responsibility for our choices creates more space and reduces the chances of us becoming resentful for finding ourselves doing things we don't want to do, or for not living the life we desire. And in order to be able to take responsibility for our choices, we need a healthy portion of selfishness and an ability to recognise our greatness, our strengths and what we bring to the table.

6. Think like an entrepreneur

Having an entrepreneurial mindset is a way of thinking that enables us to overcome challenges, be decisive and accept responsibility for our outcomes. It is a constant need to improve our skills, learn from our mistakes and question everything. Rather than thinking *outside* the box, we should learn to think like there is no box.

Business consultant Mike Patterson encourages us to question everything and to activate our minds. He explained, 'We are told there's a pie. It's this big and your slice of the pie is this much. And if you want more you're being greedy – you're taking from somebody else.' But, he points out, if we were to search for, say, two people who look the same or who are wearing the same thing, we'd have a hard time finding them. The truth is, scarcity is a construct of the mind and there is, in fact, enough for everyone. This is because, as Mike says, we've been 'conditioned to accept what we've been told. We haven't been taught to think'.

We need to teach ourselves to think, be critical, question what we see and find answers that satisfy us. Andrea Heuston did think and, therefore, reacted intelligently when she was laid off from her team-leader position while in her early twenties. When her employers realised their mistake and asked her and her team to come back, rather than jumping at the opportunity Andrea got a business licence and negotiated her return through her own company. Andrea suggests if you 'come at everything from a position of abundance you will always have enough. So even when there's scarcity, think as if you have abundance'.

Andrea thought outside the box. Autopilot mode doesn't work for entrepreneurs and other audacious people. Neither does living a lie.

It is vital to practise speaking the truth, even if it's uncomfortable for both ourselves and others. We need to get past that if we want to lead authentic, audacious lives. Maltese singer Claire Tonna says that the more honest we are with ourselves, the better our lives will be. Unfortunately, honesty is not encouraged in our society. Claire says many people are living a lie because they're scared or they don't dare admit what they feel. People seem happy to run on autopilot.

Another way of thinking like an entrepreneur, even if we are working for others, is to dedicate part of our working week to something which fills us with passion. Leadership coach Dalia Feldheim advises companies to allow their employees to work one out of five days on their passion project. She says this gives them such an energy boost that it compensates for the more mundane tasks people do on the other days. In addition, entrepreneurial thinking is about having a sense of purpose, a growth mindset and a feeling of positivity. It's about being emotionally brave and permitting ourself to be human. Dalia says it's okay not to be okay and that having negative emotions is a good thing, as long as we acknowledge them and don't try to hide them, otherwise they may burst forth in some form of toxic behaviour or passive aggressiveness.

An entrepreneurial mindset requires an obsession with the goal. Scottish islander Kenneth Mackay possesses a special kind of perseverance. He says he's the kind of person who never gives up, even when others ridicule his stubbornness. Kenneth's arduous work and obsession with his goal eventually saved his village from abandonment.

Successful entrepreneurs embrace challenges, mistakes and failures as opportunities to develop new skills, and they learn to get comfortable being uncomfortable, by embracing risks and doing new things. Part of cultivating an entrepreneurial mindset is spending time with other entrepreneurs.

For example, Timmy Douglas finds that his success in his personal development had much to do with surrounding himself with likeminded people. Timmy explained we have a certain set of beliefs that determine our thoughts and create specific feelings from which our actions arise, and these lead to particular results. The causal relationship looks like this:

BELIEFS › THOUGHTS › EMOTIONS › BEHAVIOUR › OUTCOMES

So if we wish to change the results, then a change anywhere up the chain will create and support that change. However, committing to change can be difficult on our own. Timmy advises reaching out to people who are a couple of steps ahead of where we want to be and spending time with them, thus providing the inspiration for us to make the changes we need to make. When we do this, then anyone in our lives who is on a different path will, by default, stop wanting to be around us because we have changed and are doing new things.

Essentially, one of the most significant factors in our lives is the people around us. If we surround ourselves with negative people who rejoice in complaining, we'll eventually find ourselves feeling the same way. But if we surround ourselves with energising, inspiring people who have been where we are right now, their optimism is sure to rub off on us.

7. Have faith and trust

As humans we have egos and many other imperfections. However, there is a much greater force guiding us in our audacious goals. When we learn to trust this greater force, our lives become aligned and we recognise our true nature, despite the dark forces that are trying to drag us down. The way we view the world, our place in it and how we make sense of it is up to each individual, but if we remain strong and work together we can achieve a better world.

Ousmane Pame, who is working to revive the arid and desert-like parts of the Sahel in West Africa to the lush and abundant habitat it once was, spoke to us with an open heart about 'dark forces that are taking people's energy and resources' and concentrating the wealth in less than 1% of the world's population. Ousmane talks about creating a 'circle of friendship where people, no matter their race or where they live, can hold hands and together reinvent a new planet and a new life across borders.' Ousmane has the utmost faith and trust that this result can be achieved.

When faced with seemingly insurmountable tasks, researcher and human rights advocate Omolade Femi-Ajao puts her faith in God. In moments when she feels she can't go on and is being dragged down by dark forces, Omolade senses God is helping her rise again. She told us:

> I literally feel myself going down and then I get to a level, it's almost like a baseline. I keep going down and I think I don't want to go up now, I'm just going to look for something else. And then I hit a point and my help comes from the Lord and I start rising again.

Social justice campaigner Maryam Mohiuddin Ahmed invites us to consider Ubuntu, an African philosophy which refers to a group of values and practices that make people authentic human beings – part of a larger and more significant relational, communal, societal, environmental and spiritual world.[2] It is often summarised as 'I am because you are, and since you are, definitely I am'. So it is society that gives human beings our humanity, and humanity comes from being part of the tribe.

Singer/songwriter Claire Tonna also has the mindset of having faith and trust and of being in service and contributing to humanity. Claire spent many years working with poor people in Calcutta, where she lived from hand to mouth and, when she had no money for rent, would simply live in the forest, trusting in a bigger force of joy. Claire believes we are in this world to be happy, not to suffer, and when we accept we are here to feel alive, to be loved and to belong, we start making better decisions and are more honest with ourselves.

Like Claire, fierce life warrior and spiritual mentor Julie Trager doesn't let societal norms and pressures tell her who she is or how to show up in the world. As a result, she says her life is 'incredibly joyful and peaceful and interesting and fun' because her faith and trust have helped her understand 'how magical living an audacious life can be'. Julie has become a warrior and mentor for helping other people 'step into their own way of living a fierce life'.

Former Buddhist monk Amaranatho says freedom is our true nature and that we should trust who we are right now in this moment. He says life is created one step at a time, but we can only see the path in retrospect. And although our actions may not feel audacious at the time, those small steps become something bigger.

Professional housesitter and intrepid traveller Susanne Hillmer would agree. Susanne has learned to listen intently to her inner voice and trust her instincts to know what to do at any given moment. Susanne is constantly trying to connect her own emotions to what is happening in the outside world, in order to avoid reacting from fear and to have faith that everything will be alright.

2 | Ubuntu philosophy. (2022, August 31). In *Wikipedia*. https://en.wikipedia.org/wiki/Ubuntu_philosophy

8. Believe you can do it

Our thoughts can release abilities beyond normal limits. We can do a lot more than our body and mind say we can. Mindsets change us, so we should deliberately choose those mindsets that improve our abilities.

Marathon runner Tish Joyce went through that mindset change on her preparatory trips to run across Europe. On one trip, Tish endured painful leg injuries and was crying with every step she took, doubting whether she could actually achieve her goal. It was Tish's young granddaughter who saved the day when she exclaimed, 'You can do it, Granny!' That was the push Tish needed to change her mindset. With those words in her head, Tish stopped the negative thinking and completed her run across Europe.

Motivational speaker Terry Tucker says that when we think we are at the end of our rope, we're actually only at 40% of our maximum potential and we still have another 60% left in reserve to give. Terry says:

> *If we can control our mindset, we become what we think. Whatever you're thinking, if it's not good, change that narrative and put something positive in there.*

Gavin Scott also believes we can achieve anything we put our mind to, even if that means going beyond our means. While preparing to swim the English Channel, Gavin told us that our bodies can achieve whatever our mind believes, and that we can do things above and beyond what we may previously have thought we're capable of because, ultimately, we're superhuman.

In conclusion, our mindset affects the way we think about everything and it plays a significant role in determining our life's outcomes. By understanding, adapting and shifting our mindset, we can improve our health, decrease stress and become more resilient. Our mindset matters because it shapes the way we view the world and can therefore constrict or expand the way in which we engage with life. To continue nurturing a positive mindset, however, we need to keep our inner critic in check, which is easier said than done, as we'll find out in the next chapter.

Questions for the reader to consider

In this chapter we have identified eight main approaches to a mindset that can build the basis for living an audacious life:

Set goals
Make plans
Let go of control
Know your worth
Abandon the victim mentality
Think like an entrepreneur
Have faith and trust
Believe you can do it

If you **have already done** something audacious, which of these approaches do you feel you embodied while you were pursuing your audacious goal? Describe the mindset you nurtured in order to do the audacious thing you did.

If you **would like to do** something audacious, which of these approaches do you feel is stopping you from making a start on your audacious path? How do you feel you can overcome them and develop an audacious mindset?

Chapter Four

The Inner Critic

We think that we are one person, that there is just one version of ourselves and nothing else. Admittedly, in the material world, it seems to be that way. In our conscious mind, however, there is more than just one of us.

We come in different versions of ourselves. What we mean by that is that we choose which aspects of our personality we want to show to a particular person in a specific situation. This stems from the theory of psychologist Carl Jung, who called the 'persona' what we show to others and how we present ourselves, and the 'shadow' the part that we do not. Most often, we are unaware that the shadow even exists.

The conscious mind is able then to have different voices, some of which can be quite assertive in areas where we feel confident. For some people that might be at home communicating with our partner or children; for others, it might be at work, talking with peers or team members, or when giving presentations or participating in meetings.

There is one particular pervasive voice that is mean, unapologetic, unempathetic and even abusive. That is the voice of the inner critic: the voice of self-doubt, insecurity and fear. This is not us. Or, at least, it's not all of us. It might feel like the voice of the inner critic takes a lot of space, as if it's the only voice there is in our mind, but it's not.

This is one of the first challenges our audacious guests report they needed to overcome – to learn how to manage the inner critic. The first question that arises is 'why would anyone have an inner critic?' It sounds so counterintuitive. Business consultant Mike Patterson told us it goes back to a childhood spent in a school system that has been purposely designed to limit our creativity.

Mike informed us that, at the beginning of the 20th century, Andrew Carnegie and John D. Rockefeller decided they needed to start 'educating the population' in order to produce workers rather than thinkers. As a result, Mike says, two key components were removed from the school system: goal-setting (knowing what we want in life) and managing finances (one of the means to get there). Mike laments that what we are taught instead is that life consists primarily of going to school, getting good grades, leaving school, getting a job, earning money and paying taxes. And this is what we are told success is.

However, studies have shown that this can have a hugely detrimental effect on our levels of creativity. When we enter school, we are 98% creative. Pre-teen, this figure has already dropped to 30%, and by the time we enter adulthood it's a mere 2%.[1] In other words, we are born creative geniuses but, to quote Mike again, the school system 'dumbs us down'. Fierce life-warrior Julie Trager sums it up nicely when she says:

1 | These figures come from a study by George Land and Beth Jarman published in 1992 and summarised by Gavin Nascimento on 28 April 2017 at https://anewkindofhuman.com/creative-genius-divergent-thinking-test/

Our educational system developed around the idea that we have to create good workers who can fit into a society that works for money and then provides for themselves and their families, and much of what we teach children is simply how to live in this well-ordered society. But in order to do that, you have to tamp down a great deal of yourself. When we are born, we are so much closer to God than we are even ten years later, because by then we've lost that connection to God, to our intuition, to our own sense of self. It's been trained out of us.

It's little wonder, then, that we grow up with a voice inside us that tells us we're not good enough, not creative enough or not talented enough to do whatever we want to do. That voice has been programmed into us by a system that aims to tamp us down and keep us dumb and, as adults, it takes a lot of hard work to undo the damage to our self-esteem that we endured in our childhood. Most people don't bother. Audacious people, however, know that in order to move forward it's crucial that we deal with the demon we call our inner critic.

This little beast comes in different disguises, which include:

1. Impostor syndrome
2. Fear of failure
3. Fear of success
4. Fear of the unknown
5. Guilt

Let's take a look at these in detail and find out how our guests have been able to deal with these troublesome aspects of their own inner critics.

1. Impostor syndrome

'Who am I to be making videos? Who am I to be doing a podcast and talking about these things?' This is the voice of self-doubt that plagued Denise Cowle when she pivoted after 25 years as a physiotherapist to start her (now very successful) business as an editor and copywriter, making videos and podcasts to showcase her work.

Impostor syndrome is the internal experience of believing that we are not as competent as others perceive us to be or as expected. In other words, we feel like a phony and we worry that others might discover our incompetence.

Former marketing executive Dalia Feldheim describes impostor syndrome as the belief that our successes are external and our failures are internal. So if we fail, we believe it's because we're no good at what we're trying to do, even if the 'failing' most probably has nothing (or very little) to do with us. On the flip side, Dalia says, we externalise success, putting it down to things like 'I was lucky. I had a great team'. Dalia remembers how lucky she felt in her former job after every successful marketing assignment, until the day it dawned on her that she must have been very blessed indeed to have experienced a 17-year corporate career based on pure luck. Maybe she had something to do with her own success after all!

Lifelong learner Aurora Pérez-Vico describes her experience with impostor syndrome as the feeling that everyone else is in a better position than herself to be able to do things. When she was asked to submit an article for publication, her first thought was 'I'm not going to be able to do that. I can't write. Someone else can do it better than me'. Fortunately, Aurora conquered her fear and wrote the article, discovering afterwards that 'the world didn't explode, nothing happened, it was fine'. Aurora told us how good she felt after this achievement and that she has now learned to say yes to similar challenges in order to learn and grow.

If we don't say yes, the danger is that we will continue to find evidence to support the alternative truth we want to believe. Returning to Denise Cowle, she told us that she would always be able to think of someone else who could do the job better than her, and for that reason she would convince herself not to do it. Well, of course there is someone else who can do the job, and perhaps better than us, but that doesn't mean we shouldn't do it. Nobody can do the thing we do quite like we can!

Horse expert Katie Taylor found this out for herself when she started practising natural horsemanship at a very young age. Feeling somewhat embarrassed about this 'alternative' way of working with horses, and mistrusting her own abilities, Katie told us she would practise with her horse behind a bush so that no one could see what she was doing. After a while, she noticed that she and the horse were getting better at working together, and slowly other people started noticing too and asking her for advice on how to solve behavioural problems with their own horses.

Katie recalled an inspirational encounter she'd had a few years earlier with a wolf expert. Fascinated by the expert's depth of understanding of wolf psychology, Katie asked him how long he'd been working in this field, expecting him to say he was born a wolf lover and had grown up amongst these intriguing animals. She was surprised to find that he didn't start learning about wolves until he was in his forties and has since become a renowned expert, whose knowledge and advice is valued all over the world. This discovery really helped Katie deal with any of her own issues she may have had around impostor syndrome!

Signs that tell us we're dealing with impostor syndrome are that we:

- are unable to realistically assess our competence and skills
- attribute our success to external factors
- are afraid of not living up to expectations
- criticise our performance
- tend to be overachievers
- are plagued by self-doubt

• set very challenging goals and then feel disappointed when we don't reach them.

This triggers a vicious cycle in which we think the only reason we were successful at something is because we overprepared. Therefore, experiencing a positive outcome might not change our intrinsic belief that we are not good at something. If we received this feedback very early in our life, which is highly likely, our core beliefs won't change, even if we have the data to prove ourselves wrong.

Denise is resigned to the fact she'll probably be dealing with impostor syndrome all her life. Her strategy is to focus on the doing and not on the result. She says she has reached a point in her life where she now thinks, 'I'll just do it, what's the worst that can happen? If it doesn't work, I'll do something else.'

Musician and composer Colin O'Donohoe has a similar way of dealing with his inner critic. While accepting the result may not be what he was aiming for, like Denise he focuses on the action. Colin believes that the only way to fight our 'demons' is to *do*. He told us:

> So I just sit down and compose. Sometimes I compose amazing stuff and sometimes I compose crap. It doesn't matter – I compose something.

We are not impostors. We are here to do the thing we are meant to be doing, and we have all we need in order to be able to do that thing. Impostor syndrome is only that – a syndrome. It doesn't exist except in our heads. When we understand where it came from, what it looks like and why it's there, we can begin to do something about it.

2. Fear of failure

A second aspect of the inner critic is being afraid of failing or of making mistakes. This can be the result of, for example, being a perfectionist or suffering from anxiety. What we are doing is avoiding engaging in new situations or taking up new challenges because we feel anxious, helpless or powerless and, in general, that we have a loss of control.

Some of the characteristics of fear of failure overlap with impostor syndrome, such as underestimating our abilities, believing we don't have the skills and worrying that others are better than us or that we will disappoint them. One thing that people who suffer from fear of failure do is procrastinate, lower their expectations or tell others they will probably fail.

In our conversations, we found that those guests who were aware of their fear of failure had developed different strategies to cope with them to avoid letting the fear take control. These are some of the strategies we learned about:

The first is to reframe the meaning of failure, in other words, change the *meaning* the word 'failure' has for us. For example, award-winning entrepreneur and CEO Andrea Heuston calls it 'failing forward'. Andrea says that if something doesn't work, it's not the end of the world: 'You learn and you move on and you take that lesson and make yourself and your company and your strategy better because of it.'

Organisational psychologist Dalia Feldheim told us about a 'graveyard of projects' she saw on a visit to the headquarters of a large tech company. She said that for every failed project the relevant team performs a 'fail forward analysis' in order to understand what they learned from the 'failure' and how they intend to make sure it doesn't happen again. Dalia said this how they encourage their employees to try, to dare and to be audacious, adding, 'You miss 100% of the shots you don't take.'

Business consultant Mike Patterson reframes failure as 'feedback'. He says we come out of school so afraid of failing that we won't even try. Mike prefers not to use the word 'fail' at all, instead saying that when we have a plan which we carry out but don't get the results we expect, then what we get is feedback. Either our plan was wrong or the way we carried it out was wrong, so we just change what was wrong. There's no failing about it.

A second strategy is to face the fear, focus on doing things and give ourself the opportunity to try out new things, seeing it more as an experiment that can go either way. Aurora Pérez-Vico mentioned how important it is for her to say yes to more things. Even when she is not sure what the outcome will be, she's willing to give it a try. She says it's never going to be a perfect time, but 'it's all about saying yes to new things and exploring new paths'.

Career transition coach Myah Payel Mitra is convinced that the fear of failure kills more dreams than failure itself. She recommends making allies with our fear. Myah told us:

> It's almost like having a friend – like you invite that friend for a cup of coffee and a chat and ask, 'What is it that you're here for?'

She rightly points out that fear is just a feeling and advises giving it the chance to express itself. 'You have a chat, an answer will come. And that is the time you have to listen.'

Primary school teacher Nik Pandya calls this being a witness to his thoughts. He said that, instead of ignoring the voice that criticises and puts him down, he listens. And the more he listens, the more he sees how those ideas are not helpful. The result is that the voice gets quieter because it's not getting the reaction it wants. Nik referenced a talk given by American researcher and academic Brené Brown, in which she compared life to being either a spectator in the seats or a player in the arena, and asked us what we would prefer to be.[2] When Nik gets negative thoughts, he reminds himself it's just the spectator criticising and he would much prefer to be in the arena.

2 | 'The Man in the Arena' speech is originally by Theodore Roosevelt and is quoted in Brené Brown's *Daring Greatly: How the Courage to be Vulnerable Transforms the Way We Live, Love, Parent and Lead* (Penguin, 2012)

Entrepreneur Felicia Specht faces her fears by writing them down, then asking herself, 'What's the worst that can happen?' This helps to reduce the *effect* of the fear, since facing our fear actually weakens it. It goes from being an overwhelming feeling in us that blocks us from doing what we want to do, to something specific that we can deal with.

A third thing we can do is to *plan* for our failures – to envision the possibility of 'failing' and to think about how we would deal with it, should things turn out that way. For example, Anne Cholawo, who gave up a hectic urban lifestyle for life on a remote Scottish island, built what she called her 'failure cop-out' into her relocation plan. She thought about how it would feel if it all went wrong and whether she could cope with that, deciding that if in the end it didn't work out, at least she would have tried it. Anne prefers doing things that way than not knowing what the outcome would have been had she been too afraid to try.

Terry Tucker says that when we look back on our lives we'll inevitably discover that the things we regret are not the things we did, but the things we didn't do, and by then it's too late to go back and do them. Terry also told us, 'I have yet to meet a successful person that hasn't experienced failure in some way or another.' He says success is paved with failure and it's all about taking personal responsibility for what we do. Quoting former South African president Nelson Mandela – who said 'I never lose, I either learn or I win' – Terry says taking personal responsibility means developing the attitude of identifying what we learned from each situation so that we can move on and grow.

3. Fear of success

Yes, there is such a thing as fear of success, even if it might sound odd. Precisely because we automatically think that everyone *wants* success – after all, that's what we've been taught – this is a hard one to spot. Fear of success involves being afraid of achievement, often to the point that we will sabotage ourselves and our efforts. We are not afraid of success itself, though; the fear is connected to the potential *consequences* of success and the idea that achieving our goals means making sacrifices or dealing with losses.

Myah said that her fear of dreaming big was a huge challenge for her. She recalled her sleepless nights where she lay thinking 'what if I tried?' Not 'what if I failed?', but 'what if I tried?' In the end, Myah decided 'let me just try and I'm going to give it my all'.

Dalia connects her fear of success with her fear of jealousy. She said our fears as adults are created in our formative years by limiting beliefs that originated in situations that occurred when our infantile brains didn't know how to handle them. Dalia's limiting belief was that being too successful would cause her pain, but now she understands that when we're successful we're inspiring others to also be their best by setting a bar, or giving people a roadmap of what success could look like for them.

Or, in the words of spiritual thought leader Marianne Williamson:

> Our deepest fear is not that we are inadequate. Our deepest fear is that we are powerful beyond measure. It is our light, not our darkness that most frightens us. And as we let our light shine, we unconsciously give other people permission to do the same.[3]

4. Fear of the unknown

A fourth aspect of the inner critic that we identified from our conversations is the fear of not knowing what might happen as a result of our actions. This is connected to our inability to predict

3 | https://marianne.com/

outcomes and to being unsure of how things will develop.

According to life coach Rebecca Allen, fear stems from a lack of knowledge. Rebecca's approach is to do research in order to fill the information gaps. She recommends we start with a vision of the ultimate thing we want and then work out the steps needed to make it happen, all the while plugging our knowledge gaps by being curious about learning those steps. Rebecca says the more we learn, the less scary it seems. If we let our fear overtake us when we don't have enough information in our hands, the *fear* becomes the knowledge, rather than the knowledge becoming the knowledge, meaning we make our decisions based on fear instead of on the facts or the research that we've done in the curiosity phase.

In fact, Terry Tucker, who has come up with ten principles for leading an uncommon and extraordinary life, told us the principle that resonates with him above all is 'most people think with their fears and their insecurities instead of using their minds'.

Angela Papalia, who left a busy law practice in urban Ontario, Canada, and switched to working remotely from a pueblo in Mexico, is perhaps a prime example of this. Angela says that in all her jobs she probably stayed longer than she should have because of the fear of not knowing what would happen if she left. Angela told us that relocating to Mexico was scary and difficult for her, because she was worried about finding her own clients. However, when she did finally make the move, her clients went with her. It was then that Angela made the conscious decision to stop worrying about money. She says she'll find some way of working for the rest of her life and that, even at a relatively young age, she's already considering several jobs she could do when she's ready to retire.

Editor and proofreader Denise Cowle told us she wanted to study English at university but she had no concept at the time of what she would do with a degree in that subject. She said, 'The fear of that unknown, of coming out with a degree and not knowing what to do, stopped me from doing that.' Denise studied a more 'practical' subject and worked as a physiotherapist for 25 years, admitting that, in that time, her fear of the unknown probably stopped her from doing a lot of things. When she realised she was moving through life at quite a speed, and if she didn't do what she wanted to do now she would probably regret it forever, this gave Denise the push she needed to get over her fear and make the career switch. Ironically, she ended up working in a job in which English language skills are paramount.

We get stuck trying to visualise the whole journey and what the outcome looks like, whereas if we act on our intuitions, the details will take care of themselves. The outcome may not be exactly what we planned, but ultimately it will be the right one.

5. Guilt

Anger, guilt and discomfort are emotions most of us have experienced. We need to remember, though, that emotions are simply feelings that evoke physiological symptoms in our bodies and conditioned thinking patterns in our minds.

Emotions are neither good nor bad, they just are. Admittedly, some emotions are more uncomfortable than others, and we have learned to attach negative meanings to some, but continuing to do that will serve us little. It's far more beneficial to be honest with ourselves, name whatever it is that we're sensing, and let that feeling be. Eventually, all feelings come and go if we don't resist and cling to them. In order to move on to our next audacious goal, we need to make peace with our emotions, especially those that are rooted in fear. If we don't make peace with them this time, they'll come back bigger next time.

One very touching story we heard was from Lynn Yap, who was working as an investment banker in New York. Lynn learned that her grandmother in her native Malaysia was critically ill and didn't have long to live, so she asked her boss for time off to be with her family. Her boss refused, saying it would jeopardise the business deal they were currently working on. Lynn described herself as being torn between her duty to her work and her family, and ultimately she chose to stay in New York. She told us that for a long time afterwards she felt guilt, shame and anger for the choice she made not to spend that time with her family and bid farewell to her grandmother, and she wasn't able to speak about the episode for many years. However, it did cause Lynn to think about her values, and she ended up leaving her banking career and switching to voluntary work mentoring entrepreneurs. Lynn told us she's finally been able to make peace with what happened and is sharing her story and using her experience to help others deal with their own inner critics and feelings of guilt.

For Maribel, turning down the volume of the inner critic was of paramount importance for her self-improvement. The voice of the inner critic was connected with a guilt that stemmed from her childhood when people reacted negatively to what she said or did, especially in her most intimate relationships. Two things helped her start to change. First of all, deflecting the responsibility of how people reacted to what she said back to the owner of said reaction; if a person gets angry because of something she says, it is their personal choice to react with anger. Everyone can choose how they react to what happens around them. The second thing is to reframe her perception of expressing her desires. It's not a complaint or imposition, it's simply speaking her truth.

Psychologist Charlene Camilleri Duca also felt guilt when she decided she wanted to travel around Europe for several months with her family. She told us she felt a responsibility to the people around her, especially her co-workers and clients, and was worried that they may have thought she didn't care about them. Charlene dealt with this by giving herself permission to say she can still be there for others while at the same time doing something that allows her to feel alive. She admits she sometimes feels like she gives too much of herself and ends up sacrificing a lot of her time and energy for others, but what she found when she voiced her fears was that most people were very supportive of her decision. Charlene says it took a lot to overcome her feelings of guilt and to say 'I trust that people are going to be okay, that I'm going to be okay, and that I can do this'.

Charlene believes we are our own worst critics, and that if we test our fears with reality, inevitably it's never as bad as we thought. We tend to make assumptions about what other people are thinking when if we simply enter into conversation with them, we'll find out the truth. Essentially, there is nothing to fear but fear itself.

A final word on the inner critic

We must be very careful not to give our inner critic space and allow self-doubt to grow, warns musician and composer Colin O'Donohoe. He says the inner critic is far more damaging than the outer ones. The latter plant the seeds in our brains for self-doubt to grow, but those seeds will only grow if we give them energy and attention. Colin suggests that

> *instead of fighting those weeds and trying to pull them out of our brains, it's better to plant seeds of positivity and water those. The negative weeds are always going to be there but, hopefully, our positive ones over time grow taller and take more of the sunlight, and the bad ones start to diminish.*

Now that we know how to deal with the negative weeds nurtured by the inner critic, let's find out how to handle the seeds planted by those irksome outer critics.

Questions for the reader to consider

In this chapter we have identified five ways the inner critic can make itself known:

Impostor syndrome
Fear of failure
Fear of success
Fear of the unknown
Guilt

If you **have already done** something audacious, did any of these come up for you while you were pursuing your audacious goal? If so, how did you deal with them?

If you **would like to do** something audacious, are any of these coming up for you while you are considering making a start on your audacious path? If so, how do you feel you can deal with them?

Chapter Five

Outer Critics

A s if the inner critic wasn't bad enough, many of our audacious guests also had to deal with interrogation from others, be they close friends and family or complete strangers. The feedback they encountered ranged from genuine incomprehension to very harsh criticism and appeared to be caused by three main factors:

- Concern for the welfare of the audacious person (from friends and family)
- Cultural bias leading to differences of opinion (from wider circles)
- Malicious intent, possibly stemming from fear or envy (from others)

So how do we deal with such reactions, particularly the hurtful ones, and particularly from those people who are close to us and whose opinions we value? This is what our guests said:

Dealing with questions from friends and family

Most of the feedback from friends and family tended to be based on genuine concern for the welfare of the audacious person. People's reactions are based on their own conditioning and understanding of the world, and friends and family often can't grasp the choices we make. As a result, their automatic response is to think we're crazy. So how do we deal with that? One way is to allow the other person to have a taste of the life you've chosen.

Rika Cossey, who moved with her young family into a tiny house on a Swedish farm in her quest to lead a life of self-sufficiency, told us that her family couldn't fathom what they were trying to do and why they would want to live in a tiny house. Rika recalls her mother asking her why they don't live in a 'real' house, and she found such questions difficult to answer. She said that explaining her decisions without first having the acceptance of others wasn't easy but she managed it with patience, with facts, and with action – when Rika's mum came to visit, Rika put her up in their tiny house.

Not all reactions from friends and family are negative – there is often a balance. With a similar intention to Rika's, Anne Cholawo moved to a very isolated location on a small Scottish island without access to public transport or other modern amenities. Anne told us she experienced mixed reactions from her work colleagues in the city and from her friends and family. Her sister thought she was crazy, and others accused her of running away from the world, which Anne admits she probably *was* doing, at least from a world she no longer wanted to be part of. Anne recalls how her new neighbours reacted to her arrival on the island:

> They thought I was mad. They probably gave me six months at the most. They couldn't understand why I was there and what I intended to do once I was there, and I have to give them credit that they be-

haved very well towards me, considering that they had no expectation of me making it at all.

Fortunately, others were more forgiving. Anne explains, 'I had an aunt who was very positive, who said, "Well, if that's what you want to do, just go and do it".' Anne still lives on the island, more than 30 years later.

Angela Papalia also received mixed reactions from friends and family when she decided to leave her full-time job in a law practice in Canada and move to a small town in Mexico. Angela says some people were very supportive and promised to visit her but others raised concerns about what the move would do to her career or whether her new location was a safe place to live. She says some of her less-supportive friends have since come around, but one of her friends revealed the real depth of her anxieties. Angela told us, 'One friend said, "I need you here",' to which Angela responded, 'I'm sorry, but I can't make my life decisions on what you need. What about if I said, "I need you here"?'

The problem is, we tend to be more affected by negative reactions, so if we're not 100% convinced ourselves of what we're doing, there's a danger we'll be adversely influenced by those. The key to dealing with this is to sit with oneself and find out if we really are ready for this choice. Ultimately, it's us taking the decision and therefore reaping the benefits or facing the consequences.

This is what Myah Payel Mitra did when she left a well-paid corporate job in the city to set up her own business as a movement therapy practitioner and career transition coach in rural India. At the point where she was considering making the move, she asked her family for their opinion. Myah recalls feeling depressed and dejected when her family told her she was crazy and that she wouldn't be able to make money from her new profession. She took these concerns on board and accepted that the time wasn't perhaps right for her. Myah explains that, in hindsight,

> I wasn't prepared enough to take the leap of faith back then. And when I went inside of me to really understand what it meant, that was a turning point. I decided finally that I was now ready to quit the corporate career and the hustle and bustle of living in a big city and move to a small village in India.

Primary school teacher Nik Pandya has found a method that works for him in seeking the opinions of friends and family. Initially he would avoid sharing his thoughts with them because he didn't want to hear their negative comments, but now Nik counts himself lucky that he has people around him who are not afraid to interrogate his ideas or even hurt his feelings. He admits he needs 'reality checks' in order to stay grounded in his vision and, especially if his visions are huge and he's feeling alone, he appreciates receiving constructive criticism from the people around him, even if that may mean going back to the drawing board. But he gives a word of advice: feedback and criticism have to be reciprocated. If you expect your friends to believe in you, then you have to believe in them as well, and be prepared to question their choices. Nik says:

> This kind of collaboration with your friends and family on supporting each other, whatever it is that people are going through, provides a grounding, and people forget they have access to friends and family that can offer that.

In a similar vein, Felicia Specht also sought out the opinions of trusted friends and family before she decided to leave her corporate job and start her own company. When she asked people what they thought of her business idea, she said the answers couldn't have been more black and white. This polarity of reactions forced Felicia to examine her doubts and conclude that she was the one making this decision and, therefore, she was the only one who would need to deal with the outcomes, be they negative or positive. Felicia gives some very good advice about considering the *role* we play in the lives of our friends and family, as this will help explain where their questions and doubts are coming from. She told us:

> It was very useful to listen to both [sides] and take them seriously, but also to analyse, 'Okay, where does this person know me from? Am I a daughter? Am I a younger sister? Am I a friend – an older friend, a younger friend?' It very much depends on what kind of role you play in those people's lives. Are they trying to protect you? Are they inspired by you? Those questions are important to ask yourself, so you can understand their answers better.

Felicia goes on to say, 'You can draw inspiration from so many great people out there, so don't expect your friends and family to be the best source for this.'

This is a sentiment shared by Colin O'Donohoe, who founded an orchestra of musicians from all over the world. Colin makes it very clear what he thinks about asking friends and family for advice:

> Family members or your best friends are not your target audience. So, while they love you, and probably because they do love you, they give horrible advice. They're not saying it to be mean. They're just not your target audience. Don't put a lot of value on the negative things your brother, your kid, your mom, your neighbour, your best buddy since you were five [say], don't put so much importance on that.

Similarly, Maltese singer/songwriter Claire Tonna advises trusting our own intuition over the opinions of others, no matter how difficult and potentially isolating that may be. Claire says that, ultimately, only *we* are responsible for how we live our lives, and when we experience turbulent emotions *we* are the ones who have to deal with that, not others.

Claire believes we should develop the mindset of not caring what other people think, since their thoughts are often based on their own fears. And although she acknowledges that persevering with our work on our own can sometimes feel lonely, she feels this is a sacrifice worth making. Claire told us, 'Many times I feel like a solitary wolf. I feel so invisible. So there is a cost as well, but it's worth it, because inside me I am at ease.'

Claire said she struggled much more when she was trying to fit, to bend, to belong, to be accepted, to be seen, to be loved and to get people to understand things from her perspective. Now she realises how impossible a task this is, and that we have a responsibility to ourselves not to engage in such harmful activities, even if that means sometimes feeling alone.

One final way of dealing with input from friends and family with good intentions is to set boundaries. Although the comments that Jessa de la Morena had to face were not actually criticisms of her audacious goal, the example she provides presents a useful technique for dealing with criticism that may be unintentionally harsh. Jessa battled cancer twice, which led her to start a community for people to share transformational stories and connect with others who have lived through similar experiences. Sometimes, Jessa simply wasn't ready to receive some of the 'support' that people wanted to offer. Her strategy for dealing with this was to stop the other person mid-flow and ask:

> Is what you're about to say going to make me feel uplifted and inspired? Because I really need to feel that way right now. I very much appreciate you being here for me but please, if it's not going to inspire and uplift me, could we leave that conversation for another time when I can listen to you better? Right now, I need to be uplifted.

Jessa told us she had to set boundaries for the sake of survival and to avoid feeling miserable while going through her experience. So she started the community U Are the Hero in order to be around people that were interested in transforming for the better.

Dealing with reactions stemming from cultural differences

Some of our guests who chose to do their audacious work in another country had the added difficulty of coming up against other people's cultural conditioning. Cultural programming gives us different perspectives on things, which is not a bad thing in itself but often leads to the default reaction of judging negatively those things we don't understand or are outside our repertoire of behaviours and habits. This can lead to confusion, misunderstanding and confrontation.

For example, we spoke with two Spanish women, Nahia Orduña and Aurora Pérez-Vico, both of whom are raising young children while working full-time in the south of Germany. They both experienced criticism from other women who have different opinions on the role of the mother in child-raising, a term known as 'mom-shaming'.

Neither Nahia nor Aurora can understand what the problem is, since in Spain it's quite normal for young mothers to continue working full time after having children. In contrast, German culture and maternity laws mean that if a woman were to have a baby every three years, she would be supported by the state and therefore wouldn't 'have' to work for almost ten years. Nahia's reaction when she learned about this was, 'Seriously?! What are you talking about? I mean, I was doing my MBA while I was pregnant! I was not showing any sign of giving up anywhere.'

Nahia found that she had to spend a lot of time justifying her actions to others, and she became so frustrated with the criticism that she joined professional networks to support other mothers in her local area who may otherwise not have the confidence to work while raising young children. Nahia told us:

> In the beginning I was shocked, but that turned to frustration and annoyance. The daycare person would ask, 'Are you really going to leave your child here so long? She's not even a year old!' And I was thinking, firstly, why am I being judged and secondly, why is it only me and not her father?

Nahia believes that when external critics are applying pressure for us to change our behaviours we have to be very confident of what we're doing in order to be able to resist that. Thankfully, Nahia herself possesses that confidence, but she was concerned about other women whose doubts may result in them not having a fulfilling job or realising their potential. She feels that this is actually detrimental to society, as we can lose a lot of talent that way.

Nahia's motivation comes from her desire to leave a better world for her two daughters, a world in which they can be independent and can do the work they want. In talking about her support network to help the women around her who she saw were giving up, Nahia says, 'Now these women are working again, they are very happy, they feel much more fulfilled and their life at home is also better. This is what gives me energy.'

Indeed, we need a solid sense of self, and conviction in our decisions, to be able to withstand the naysayers and negative criticism. Respecting that different people make different choices for their own reasons, and that we are standing our ground because we are in a different place in our own life's journey, gives us the permission to do what we need to do in our own way. This is how Aurora Pérez-Vico views such comments. Aurora told us:

> I try to switch off this kind of criticism and think about what's good for me and what's good for my family. If it works for us and we are good with that, then it's fine. Other people have their own way to do

things. Maybe they love to stay home with their kids. It's fine, I respect that. I like my job, I love to do things outside my home – office is 100% office, and home is 100% home.

Environmental lawyer Farhana Yamin, who moved from Pakistan to the UK at the age of eight, was the first girl in her family to go to university. She told us how her parents had to justify her decision to the local Asian community, assuaging their culture shock by reassuring them she would be living with women. After finishing her degree, Farhana then proceeded to contravene another societal norm by marrying a Jew at a time when mixed race marriages were uncommon. Farhana talked about breaking barriers and using hard work and study as an escape valve and a way to navigate her path in a foreign country and language. Whatever the reactions of the Asian community around her, Farhana was determined to follow this path.

Dealing with hurtful or malicious criticism

One of the most difficult kinds of criticism to deal with is that aimed at projects which benefit the community, and in which some of our guests selflessly invested their time, energy and money to set up. Imagine you discover that something crucial is missing in your community and you take steps out of the goodness of your heart to plug that gap. How would you then feel if complete strangers claimed you were only doing it for the money or for prestige, or that your work was a load of rubbish?

This is the type of criticism that South Africa-based Mark Matamisa faced when he and his colleagues set up a project to supply safe, treated drinking water to people in his homeland of Zimbabwe, since the relevant authorities were not providing this service and it was leading to widespread disease and even fatalities. Mark was shocked by some of the negative comments he received, which were possibly coming from a place of fear or envy, but he found a strategy to deal with them.

Mark told us, 'Some of the criticism was quite eye-opening. People were questioning why we, as an entity, felt that we could charge somebody else money for water.' Mark and his colleagues had never considered this question, since the project arose out of their concerns and shared experiences of what was needed.

Further criticism came from people who called Mark's work a vanity project, claiming 'here are people who are outsiders not based in the country who have chosen to do a project to make themselves feel good and raise their profile'. Mark found it challenging to manage those perceptions. He felt he and his colleagues were 'just a group of people that wanted to serve other people like ourselves'.

He dealt with the criticism by explaining to people that the enterprise is entirely self-funded, the infrastructure they are developing is not free, and Mark and his partners do not have unlimited resources or deep pockets. Whether that assuages the outer critics remains to be seen.

Kenneth Mackay faced similar criticism during his campaign to get a road built into his remote Scottish island village. He explained that most people supported his vision of securing the future of his village, but one or two in positions of 'authority' were dead against it. Although forced to deal with one vociferous local councillor, who argued, 'What a waste of money! Why are you spending that kind of money on a dying community?', it didn't stop Kenneth continuing his fight for what he believed in. When the road was finally opened after more than a decade of campaigning, Kenneth explained that, while the community celebrated, the councillor was 'so angry that I had won'.

Our critics undoubtedly have different values than us, and that's their reason for criticising. And especially with modern technology such as social media and other platforms, it's very easy for people to shoot off comments anonymously without having the full information and without being responsible for the consequences of what they say. Whatever we do, someone, somewhere will find fault with it, and we have to learn to be okay with that.

This was a lesson that Debbie Levitt learned when she set herself the audacious goal of trying to fix the UX industry. Debbie hosts a popular video channel and is very active on social media, which of course attracts criticism like bees to honey. As well as people blocking her on these platforms, Debbie says there are others who battle her and her ideas, sometimes by writing poor reviews about her books. She likes to say that if 85% of people agree with 85% of what she suggests, it's all worth it. She doesn't expect everyone to agree with everything she believes in, but she's hoping to create a movement of people who will care more about their UX work. That is her ultimate aim.

Marketing executive Dalia Feldheim faced a type of criticism that is unfortunately only too common for those working in companies (and may be one reason why many of us choose the entrepreneurial path) – that of a toxic boss. Dalia told us she went from giving 200% in her previous job to performing at 10% of her potential, simply because she needed the rest of her energy to be able to defend herself. Dalia stayed in this company for three years, believing she could coach herself out of this toxic environment and even change her boss's behaviour but, after becoming quite sick, she left corporate life after almost two decades and started her own consultancy. She's turned her situation around and now works with individuals and companies to help them bring purpose and joy to the workplace.

Strategies for dealing with *any* kind of external criticism

The previous three sections of this chapter have given examples of typical instances where criticism can arise and how our guests dealt with them. This last section gives valuable advice from some of our guests on how to deal with outer critics, regardless of where they come from or what their intentions are.

Maryam Mohiuddin Ahmed advises staying true to our own inner voice. She says, 'The minute you start listening to your inner voice, it becomes clear that these other voices don't deserve a space.' Maryam says the naysayers don't matter anymore because there's something *we* know that they don't, which is fine because it's not their time to know right now. When it *is* their time, they *will* know.

This is not to say we should treat the naysayers in an arrogant or dismissive way because 'these people don't know better', but graciously, simply because we see our own roles in the bigger picture more clearly than others do. Once we get to this place, Maryam says we find incredible peace and that the critical comments don't bother us anymore. In fact, she says that 'sometimes, if you're lucky, they come back and say "Oh my God, that was amazing. You were right and we should have listened to you!"'.

When Julie Trager faces criticism at a human level, she turns to the spiritual world for strength. Julie says she feels showered with so much unconditional love from higher dimensions that it has helped her not only to love herself but also to appreciate that we are all on our own individual paths. Julie can now show up as her own audacious, authentic self and graciously honour everyone else who is doing what they have to do on their own life journeys, without allowing their critical comments to affect her.

Susanne Hillmer, who lives a life on the road financed by offering online training, has changed her strategy for dealing with outer critics from hiding her nomadic lifestyle to treating it as 'normal'. Susanne told us that in the beginning she often didn't mention her continually changing location to her clients, telling them simply that she was 'travelling at the moment.' Now, however, she says it's become normal to talk about her way of living and that, in fact, 'even my customers in big companies are interested and when they see me – the first thing they ask is "Where are you? Can you open your camera? Tell us something about where you are".'

Susanne has learned that the more normally she treats her lifestyle, the more normally others view it and, in doing this, she has in fact become a role model for some people. She says some of her online clients now say to her, 'You're working from a camper? Really?! This is my big dream! We have to talk. I want to know more.'

Singer/songwriter and animal rights activist Jen Armstrong has learned that, of course, other people's perceptions of the world won't always be in alignment with her own, but she has nevertheless developed the strength and courage to lead the life she wants. Jen questions the 'truths' that others live by, and if they don't make sense to her she digs deep to find out why. This empowers her to feel secure and strong in her inner voice and to be able to deal with any negativity, and even anger, against her points of view. Jen says:

> *All I've ever done is move with the best intentions, so I don't really understand this hostility towards a compassionate point of view.*
> *I find it hard to truly empathise, because if somebody had a different opinion to me, if I could see they were moving with the best intentions, then I'd want to be educated, or inspired, by it. I want to have discussions because that's how we grow and that's how we learn.*
> *I stand up for what I believe and I really believe in the truth that I hold in my heart, but I want to hear from other people and hear their perspectives as well.*

Jen reminds us to acknowledge that everybody's situation is different, and that we need to develop empathy and compassion for other people's stories and points of view. She says that, in most cases, it isn't a 'one-size-fits-all, black-and-white situation' and that 'sometimes people have to do things they wouldn't necessarily do in an ideal world'. Keeping this in mind enables us to listen intently and take part in more positive conversations and debates.

Indeed, motivational speaker Terry Tucker advises people to follow their heart and soul, despite what other people say. Terry's response to the question 'What will people say about me if I fail?' is 'Who cares?! Who cares what other people will say about you?' Since we all have unique gifts and talents, why should we care what other people think? Terry's advice is:

> *Use your gifts and talents and go after what you want because life doesn't owe you a thing. And it won't give you anything. It will fight you every single step of the way, which means you've got to have the resolve to keep going when you butt up against those impediments that we all do in our lives.*

And that includes those pesky outer critics!

Questions for the reader to consider

If you **have already done** something audacious, how did other people react to the audacious thing you did? How did you deal with their reactions?

If you **would like to do** something audacious, how do you feel other people will react to the audacious thing you want to do? How will you deal with their reactions? Do their opinions matter to you?

Chapter Six

Challenges

S o far, we've established that audacious people do what they are being called to do, whether this is triggered by a specific event or not. They also have a particular mindset and they learn to overcome their inner critics, while also deflecting worries and concerns from friends, family and other people as they continue on their audacious path.

It would be folly, however, to suggest that once those initial stages are overcome, the audacious journey is all plain sailing. Far from it. Challenges appear on the way and, like the river seeking the path of least resistance around the fallen boulder, audacious people look at challenges and calmly assess how best to go around, over or under them in their quest to achieve their ultimate goal.

Business consultant Mike Patterson told us that challenges come our way not to block us, but to help us grow, not to *ob*struct but to *in*struct. He says that when we have a goal, three things happen:

- The world checks if we are serious about our goal by putting an obstacle in the way. If we quit, the world knows we're not serious.

- If we *are* serious, the world sends us a lesson because there's a certain knowledge we need in order to move forward.
- If we don't learn our lesson the first time round, it will come back bigger. And every time we don't learn the lesson, it comes back bigger.

So, what were some of the obstacles that the world put in the way of our audacious guests in order to teach them valuable lessons and give them the relevant knowledge to move forward? More importantly, what can *we* learn from the challenges faced by others which might aid us in our own audacious journeys?

Let's take a look at some of these challenges and then assess what we can learn from them. We've found that these challenges fall into five main categories — financial, technical, psychological, physical and systemic.

Financial Challenges

Omolade Femi-Ajao is a university researcher working to improve access for ethnic minority women to health, social and community services in the UK. Research costs money, and Omolade has to continuously apply for grants in order to fund her critical work. No matter how many rejections she receives, she never gives up, although she admits this thought does occasionally cross her mind. The lesson she has learned is that her work is perhaps not on everyone's radar now, but, if she persists, she believes that one day someone somewhere will respond to her application and award her the appropriate funding. In the meantime, she's extremely grateful for whatever small amount of grant money she does manage to secure.

LEARNING POINT
Be persistent. Make the most of what you do have.

Cecilia Chiolerio started a company which offers cafés, bars and restaurants that are not usually open during the day to people seeking quiet and welcoming workspaces. She says one of her main challenges was convincing lenders or venture capitalists to invest in her idea. Cecilia told us, 'We can have all the ideas we want, but if we run out of money the business cannot go on. And when you raise money, you have to convince other people.' Like Omolade, Cecilia also receives a lot of rejections from people she feels are judging her, and she has to work hard on presenting a coherent and attractive case for why people should invest in her business.

LEARNING POINT
Know your business. Be completely confident in your ideas.

When Jen Taylor and her husband decided to take off with their family of five in a campervan for a year, they needed to plan their finances carefully. Jen continued to work at her teaching job while on the move, and they also set themselves a budget of €10 per person per day, which was managed very ably by their teenage son. Jen explains:

> We were really grounded by our 13-year-old accountant. He was the bookkeeper and every time we went out, he said, 'Have you spent any money?' And I would go, 'No, no.' 'Did you have a coffee?' 'Oh yes, sorry, I did have a coffee.' So he was great. He kept us financially grounded.

LEARNING POINT
Set budgets and stick to them.
Look for alternative income sources.

Vicky Arundel founded a yoga therapy practice offering one-to-one yoga specifically tailored to each individual's body, lifestyle and health needs, which the popular model of yoga classes involving large groups of people doesn't address. Vicky's financial challenge involved assessing what to charge for her services. As a 'new' product, she wasn't sure what people would be willing to pay for it, so she looked at similar products, such as physiotherapy and counselling, and based her rates on that. However, she says, 'That has been a challenge to work through, just to get people to think this is something worth spending money on.'

LEARNING POINT
Know the value of what you're doing and charge appropriately.

Technical Challenges

Returning to Jen Taylor and her campervan, she named two further challenges, which were more technical in nature. One of them was the administration side of things, such as sorting out the children's education, insurance, visa requirements and so on. Jen told us that, little by little, they simply worked their way through them. A bigger challenge was what to do with all the animals the family would be leaving at home. It was only at the last minute that a solution to this conundrum appeared:

> As it turned out, and not as planned, people we had couchsurfed with a couple of years before said they would housesit for us, which meant we had not only the housesitters but also animalsitters. .

LEARNING POINT
Keep calm. Solutions have a way of presenting themselves.

Technical challenges on a somewhat larger scale faced Mark Matamisa when he and his colleagues decided to set up an enterprise to provide safe, treated drinking water to families in Zimbabwe. Mark highlighted a number of issues, including: finding appropriate sites that could provide 24-hour access to the water tanks; ensuring the technology and infrastructure were safe and effective; and keeping the tanks stocked with clean water so they didn't run out or become contaminated. Mark's solution and, in his opinion, one of the best strategic decisions he and his colleagues made, was to site their tanks at fuel stations, where 'the forecourt is always open and there's always somebody to assist people who come in'.

LEARNING POINT
Research the options. Call on strategic partners for help.

Helen also faced technical challenges when she realised her dream of living in a whitewashed stone cottage with a thatched roof was probably not going to come to fruition. So she sat down and re-assessed her goal, amending it in order to make it achievable under the new circumstances. As it turned out, the home Helen bought was much more practical than the one she'd set her sights on, and in fact presented a whole new range of opportunities when she realised she could offer it as a B&B to guests wishing to get away from it all.

LEARNING POINT
Be prepared to adapt your goal in light of new developments.

Psychological Challenges

We found that some of the biggest challenges facing our audacious guests were psychological ones. Humans are complicated creatures, and if we're not beating ourselves up about the choices we make then we're having to deal with the reactions of others to them. Some of these points were mentioned in the chapters on the inner critic and outer critics, but we'd like to mention specific examples of the psychological challenges that our guests faced when setting out on their audacious journeys. We'll address these as questions to be answered.

1. *What is it that you do, exactly?*

One major challenge is how to explain to others what exactly it is that we're doing. Going back to Vicky Arundel's 'new' style of yoga practice,[1] Vicky told us that her first challenge was that yoga has an identity problem. She says: 'People have their own story around what yoga is and many don't think it's for them. So one of my roles is to educate people about what it is I do.'

It's not only yoga that has an identity problem, as Colin O'Donohoe found when he started the Pangean Orchestra, an ensemble of performers and instruments from all over the world. He explained that 200 years ago orchestral music was cutting edge and, for most people, the only chance they would get in their lives to hear such music. He says that orchestral music has gone from being extremely exciting to being seen as one of the most boring forms of entertainment, lamenting that we often use it nowadays simply to help us get to sleep or for 'the Mozart Effect, to magically make our kids smarter'.

Colin's dilemma is how to infect others with his own excitement about orchestral music. His solution is to design an orchestra and music that reflects the people in the same way it did 200 years ago. He says, 'We have to make music that excites people. That's one of the reasons why I do this project.'

LEARNING POINT
Be aware that you may need to educate people about what you do.

2. *How do I know I can trust you?*

A second challenge is getting people to trust in us and in what we

---

1| It's not actually new; it's what yoga was originally about when it developed millennia ago, but this fact has unfortunately been forgotten in modern society as it doesn't present a profitable business model.

do. Vicky and Colin both mentioned the trust issue. This is what Vicky said about her yoga practice:

> It's a very vulnerable thing to lie on a yoga mat in front of somebody you don't know, to show them who you are, what you can physically do, how you're breathing. These are all very intimate acts and you can't build that trust in one session. That's something that takes a lot of time.

Colin's work in leading a global orchestra means he is often on the road, which he's found has had a negative impact on people's levels of trust. He's attempting to deal with this by establishing a core group of people who can pick up the reins when he's on his travels, so that the project is bigger than just one person and can gain momentum.

Mark Matamisa faced difficulties getting buy-in from the community for his clean drinking water project. He told us that just because a community needs a particular service, and we feel we are meeting that need, we cannot assume that everyone will be happy we are doing this. Social issues are extremely challenging.

LEARNING POINT
Building trust takes time. Create a backup to support your work.

3. *Why should I work with you/him/her?*
Perhaps related to the trust issue is the fickle nature of the human ego. Working with others who have their own problems and personal needs has proved challenging for some of our audacious guests. Back to Colin and his international orchestra:

> The other challenge that I underestimated was musicians themselves saying, 'We need to do it this way. No, we need to do it that way. We need to do whatever.' Or one musician saying, 'I'll only play if you fire that guy.' Things like that. I wasn't expecting those issues.

In Farhana Yamin's work as an international environmental lawyer, she is constantly dealing with people who have different opinions to her own. When she set up a project to bring people together in her local community to rethink their ways of living with the land and with each other, she also invited 'those people who opposed her, especially the people who don't think there is a problem in the first place, to ask them what *their* solution is for many of the problems.'

LEARNING POINT
Accept that working with others can be tricky. Put your own ego aside and learn techniques for dealing with people.

4. *Can I really do this?*

When the inner critic kicks in and we start questioning our own abilities, this can become a real challenge. Fortunately, help is available. Cecilia Chiolerio sometimes questions her business idea of using otherwise empty bars and restaurants as professional workspaces. Cecilia told us she wouldn't be able to get through those times without both the help of her business partner and the knowledge that she's serving others. On those days when she's feeling particularly vulnerable, she expresses her doubts and fears to her business partner, who gives her strength in that moment, and then those roles may switch the next time. And when Cecilia does have those black days, she says, 'I think about our customers who are really happy with what we do, and that really drives me.'

Debbie Levitt knows that her colleagues in the UX industry face similar self-doubts, telling us that people working in this industry tend to suffer from impostor syndrome and both mental and physical health issues simply because they care so much about their work. Debbie deals with this by regularly inviting a psychologist onto her live online show to take questions from her audience and help assuage their fears.

LEARNING POINT
Reach out for help. We are stronger together.

Physical Challenges

We mention in Chapter 9 the importance of keeping ourselves in good mental and physical health, so that when we show up with our audacious goals, we can be the best we can be in service to ourselves and to others. However, some physical challenges may be out of our control and we need to find ways of working around and adapting to them.

To add to the audaciousness of Colin O'Donohoe's work, he is also recognised as being legally blind. This means that, while most orchestra conductors have the score in front of them while they're conducting, Colin has to memorise the whole thing because he's unable to see it clearly. He explained that even if he composes a piece himself, that doesn't mean he can remember every single note he wrote.

Colin's impaired vision also slows him down when composing music digitally or when corresponding online and, again, he uses memorisation to work with computer software or applications. When travelling, Colin memorises how to get around, which he says is easier in larger cities, where he can, for example, learn the subway system. But in more remote places, where he's had to rely on infrequent bus services, it can be very challenging.

LEARNING POINT
Find ways of adapting to challenges
which are out of your control.

Systemic Challenges

It appears that some challenges have been purposely designed that way by the very systems and societies in which we live, and it's the job of an audacious person to work at dismantling those systems in order to create a better world for all. These challenges are clearly on a different scale to the ones previously mentioned, but if we all do what is ours to do, slowly and surely we will chip away at our broken systems and eventually fix them.

For example, in South Africa, Peter Guess described how urban areas have been strategically designed as concentric circles, where 'the inner circle would be the white people staying closest to the metropolitan, the next ring would be the coloured communities, and outside of that would be the black communities'. Peter's challenge is to dismantle these circles, which he and his partner Alistair Maigurira are attempting to achieve through economic empowerment and diversity and inclusion work.

Alistair explained that humanity is traumatised both individually and collectively, and that we can't hope to heal the problems in our communities without each of us healing ourselves first and critically assessing our privileges. Alistair and Peter's solutions are to use storytelling to help detraumatise people and to meet people where they are.

Remaining on the African continent, but describing a problem playing out all over the world, Ousmane Pame told us about the challenges he faces as founder and director of a network of eco-villages in the Sahel in West Africa. The previously verdant land of parts of the Sahel has suffered desertification through decades of poor agricultural practices, and Ousmane is one of many people now working to revive the region to the lush and abundant habitat it once was.

Ousmane told us that up to the 1970s they had completely organic food and farming practices, until their national government was persuaded by international financial organisations to dam rivers, clear forests and start using chemicals and pesticides. He said this has resulted in 'a complete ecological and socio-economic disaster in the region' and that today 'people in this area have realised what a big mistake it was to follow this so-called modern agriculture'. He bemoans the fact that people no longer have the quality and diversity of food they once had, and that not only have people been thrust into poverty, but they're also suffering from 'new' diseases, such as diabetes, hypertension and other nutrition-related illnesses.

Ousmane is dealing with these enormous challenges by raising people's awareness via education. He and his colleagues make use of TV and radio, organise events in villages, and are in constant contact with decision-makers in the community. He says:

> It's important to remind the younger generations how important wildlife and the forests are to our culture and our balance, and that this notion of well-being that the West in general sells to Africa is not totally appropriate.

Ousmane goes on to say:

> We are trying to put something delicate together so that we can move forward – a delicate balance that we as communities, as local governments, as leaders need to design so that it's widely adopted. And then this will be the seeds of real and sustainable change.

Ousmane told us that the hardest part was trying to 'change the mental and cultural paradigm so that everyone is geared to action and to sustainable practices'. He said he has succeeded in part of this goal, but other parts are still a challenge. Nevertheless, Ousmane continues to tirelessly work with neighbouring communities 'so that we can really start fighting to reverse desertification and also reinvent our present and our future'.

Philip Keay argues that one of the reasons humanity has 'fallen out of love with itself', which has perhaps led to governments being persuaded by multinational corporations to change their practices, is that the education system has been hijacked by the very people leading such an exclusive, individualistic agenda. Philip says the system that has developed over decades has sought to stamp out our innate childlike curiosity, creativity and desire to question things. He says our school systems cultivate a 'one size fits all', where the 'answers' are given to us by authority figures and we are shaped into a mould that 'best fits society'. The result is that we often don't even realise we're talented in certain areas, or we lack the confidence to fully express ourselves, and we end up complying blindly with rules that actually harm life.

Philip says the only way to break the cycle is to educate the educators. He says we are *all* educators and we *all* need to learn how to be healthy, how to learn and how to enable learning in others. Once we re-ignite our passion for learning we'll never stop, and we'll inspire others to learn with us, creating an environment in which everyone can thrive.

Gavin Scott, whose mission is to wake people up to the way we have been programmed and conditioned, thus enabling us to make life decisions from an increased level of consciousness, says it's not only our school system that is against us, citing, for example, the marketing system and the penal system as equal culprits. Gavin says that overcoming the programming is probably the greatest challenge he comes across and that 'people really need to wake up to what is going on'.

Another challenge that has crept into our societies and systems is the proliferation of technological and other diversions that people are presented with today. Julie Trager says distractions such as TV, movies, video games, social media, entertainment, alcohol and so on, are problematic because they keep us from finding out who we really are and what we really want, which ultimately leads to unhappiness and unfulfillment.

LEARNING POINT
Be aware of how much of your behaviour
stems from societal conditioning.

It's important to realise that challenges will turn up while pursuing our audacious goals. We'll finish this chapter with a quote from entrepreneur Felicia Specht, who deals with such challenges by asking herself what is the worst thing that could happen. For Felicia personally, this would be that her business would fail and she would be back in the employment market looking for a 'regular job'. But she says she would hold her head up and proclaim, 'Hi, I'm here. I had a great deal of experience in the last year. It didn't work out the way I thought and I'm back in the job pool.'

What a great attitude to embrace!

Questions for the reader to consider

If you **have already done** something audacious, what challenges did you face in pursuing your audacious goal? How did you overcome them?

If you **would like to do** something audacious, what challenges do you think you might face in pursuing your audacious goal? How equipped are you to deal with them? What do you still need to do to prepare yourself?

Chapter Seven

Role Models

The definition of a role model in the Cambridge dictionary is 'a person who someone admires and whose behaviour they try to copy'.[1] When we are young and growing up, there is often an older person whom we admire and dote on for many reasons. This can be a parent, grandparent, teacher, sibling, cousin, uncle or aunt – someone we look up to and want to be like. Some of us may do it intentionally, while others will do it without realising how influential the person is for them.

Our role models keep changing as we grow up, according to shifts in our tastes and needs. Having role models in our life is very important, and having good role models is crucial, as they influence what we do and how we eventually turn out. Positive role models influence our actions, motivate us to uncover our true potential and overcome our weaknesses, and push us to make the most out of our lives. They also play a critical role in our self-improvement, as they

1 | https://dictionary.cambridge.org/dictionary/english/role-model

give us a standard to strive for, thus serving as inspiration to discover who we are and how to be the best version of ourselves.

In Maribel's work coaching women to find their own worth and confidence, and helping them to speak up and lead more fulfilling lives, she discovered her clients had a definite lack of worthy role models. When she discussed this with Helen they both realised that many 'regular' people are doing extraordinary things but are not being showcased anywhere. This provided the initial impetus to start the AudaciousNess podcast.

During our two years of intense, courageous conversations with 41 audacious guests, our initial definition of a role model evolved. We found that a role model does not have to be another person; nature is perhaps the most perfect role model of all, and we can seek inspiration from observing animals, trees, rivers, mountains, the wind and the sun.

When we asked our guests to identify the key role models in their lives, we got a variety of responses, which we have grouped into four main categories: family members, peers, professional mentors, and nature herself. Let's take a closer look at each of these types of role models.

Family Members

Family members can have a great positive influence on children, not only through direct interactions with them but also through the examples they set with their attitudes and behaviours within the family and in the outside world. Some of our guests said it was their parents who were the most important role models in their lives.

Omolade Femi-Ajao says not only did her parents form a great team for raising their children, but they also created a nourishing and positive environment in which to grow up. Omolade recalls of her childhood spent in Nigeria:

My parents created an enabling environment for all of us to do what we wanted to do. I was never told as a young child that you can't do something, and I remember my dad saying, 'Beyond the sky's the limit.' I was very out of place – in fact I didn't realise it wasn't normal until I started interacting with people outside my immediate family, and then people started telling me I don't fit into the mould. My 'normal' was not the society 'normal'. Because as a female child you are expected to conform to certain expectations.

Terry Tucker told us how his parents taught him very early on the importance of family, and of caring, loving and supporting one another. Terry grew up in a family of three sporting boys and this is how he describes his childhood:

We were always running in a million different directions. But it was all about things that, at least from the boys' perspective, we'd love to do. Our parents were supporting us by bringing us to these games and practices, by making sure we had meals late at night when we came home from practice, by keeping our uniforms clean and things like that.

Other guests talked about their grandparents. For example, Ousmane Pame has fond memories of his grandmother and the nourishment she gave him and his siblings growing up in Senegal. He told us:

My grandmother was a real university to me and to my brothers and sisters. She had a large herd of cows and during the summer vacations we would go and help her look after her cattle. We would go far away from the village – five, six kilometres – and stay the whole day, looking at the animals grazing. When it was very hot, we'd get under the shade of a tree and my grandmother would share all these stories. She told us all the different kinds of trees, the medicinal use of herbs, etc. It was absolutely fascinating opening so many windows and doors in our small brains. Far away from the village, we had no water or food but we were fully fed and nourished with all these stories.

Felicia Specht also has great admiration for her grandmother, who, despite the conditions facing many women living and working in Germany in the mid-20th century, still managed to do very inspirational things. Felicia says of her grandmother:

She's an inspiration for me because she grew up in far more unequal and challenging times than we do and yet she managed to study, she managed to work, she did small jobs to finance her first bike to be able to travel across Germany. She was such an independent woman. Looking at what she had to face during World War II, every time getting back up on her feet with zero money, sewing her own clothes, staying strong and positive and still enjoying life. She had such an enjoyment for art, for music, for books, for flowers. To find those inspirations in life, to still see them even though horrible things happened to you and to your family, I think that's very uplifting and I can only draw from this.

Andrea Heuston was also greatly inspired by what she refers to as her amazingly strong grandmother. Andrea told us:

My grandmother had a life of bouncing forward. She lived in government housing with her two boys when my grandfather left her high and dry. So she went and got a job at this huge airplane company called Boeing. And at the time, the computers were as big as a house and she ran the computer room. So she chose how to react and how to move forward in such a way that it would be a positive experience for her family. I believe the strong females in my life, both of my grandmothers, helped me to realise that I could be whatever I wanted to be.

And Katie Taylor talked about her aunt, a natural horsemanship instructor and equine therapist, as being an inspirational role model, always ready to give her advice whenever needed.

However, not all of us find ourselves in the lucky situation of having excellent role models within our own families. Fortunately, there are plenty of other role models out there, if we go out and seek those people that give us the inspiration and the push we may need to be able to pursue our audacious goals.

Peers and other audacious people

Felicia is not only inspired by her grandmother, she also gets a lot of inspiration from her peers and colleagues in a local networking group she founded. Her group, Creative Ladies, showcases experienced women in creative industries by providing a stage for them to share their accomplishments with a small group of younger women. Felicia says it's extremely fulfilling to see how these inspiring women realise, while sharing what they have done in their lives, that their work is important, relevant and interesting to others.

In a similar fashion, Lynn Yap set up an organisation to provide role models to girls between 13 and 16 years old, who might not otherwise be exposed to women that work outside of the home. By presenting women who have successful careers in different types of jobs, Lynn aims to show young women what they are capable of aspiring to. Her message to them is that nothing is impossible.

Nahia Orduña also started a networking group in her area, as she appreciates the importance of sharing knowledge and inspiring others. In fact, Nahia told us she was inspired to publish her first book after being in contact with one of her peers who had done the same thing.

Denise Cowle told us she has admiration for her friends and colleagues, especially those from whom she feels she can learn. Denise says it's not a one-way process, though, and she gives back as much, if not more, than she gets. Under the sentiment 'a rising tide lifts all boats', Denise and her colleagues are constantly working with each other, despite also competing with each other, to be the best editors they can.

And Jen Taylor told us about the profound impact a Dutch/Canadian couple who had made their home in Spain had on her. Jen met them while on her travels, helping out on the organic farm they set up in the 1970s. She told us:

> They were really forward thinking. They had a little restaurant that served organic food before anyone was aware of environmental issues and they had a bin that was tiny at the end of the week. Water was precious because they weren't connected to the mains. Electricity was precious because they had a generator. They were incredible and they had such a profound impact on us.

Many of us are fortunate enough to have met people who have had such a profound impact on our lives. Nevertheless, there is yet another route we can take to bring role models into our awareness – by seeking out those who make it their life's purpose to help others.

Professional mentors

Professional mentors can help in our career progression, offering us valuable advice, support and assistance from their wealth of knowledge and experience. These relationships may either be formally arranged or they may develop organically due to favourable circumstances. Four of our guests talked about these types of relationships.

Cecilia Chiolerio told us her mentor is the founder of a startup she used to work at. Cecilia recalls how he gave her the confidence to set up her own business and is still there to help her analyse her ideas, make important decisions and provide support when she starts doubting herself. Comparing professional mentors with other role models, Cecilia explains:

It's not so much about having role models – that's super important. But having mentors is a game changer. Because in my day-to-day business I do so many things I don't have a clue about. And sometimes it's cool that I can figure it out on my own. And sometimes I make mistakes. But sometimes there are decisions that are way too big. And when you mess those decisions up, it's a problem. My mentor is there in exactly those moments. He's never told me what to do but he always allows me to think about the best way to approach a decision. And that's important because you save so much time and really big mistakes if you have someone you trust who knows what to do.

Nik Pandya told us about starting his teaching career in an inner-city school under difficult circumstances that required him to deal with lots of things all at once. He really appreciated the support he received from 'amazing leaders who would just take me out for a coffee sometimes when it got too much'.

Nik laments that there is so much pressure and workload in the school system nowadays that people don't have the space, time or capacity to mentor others like they used to. Either that or those mentors are not practising anymore. Nik says:

I was very fortunate to be trained by unbelievable teachers when I started off and I still call them now to say, 'Listen, I'm struggling, can you help me?' And now when I speak to them, they've all left the profession. What's happening that we're losing these great teachers? Is there a disconnect between the curriculum or the school policy to very inspirational and talented teachers and leaders?

Nik wonders whether there is time for support like that again and is working to create an educational model that will allow for that crucial mentoring network to be re-established.

When Timmy Douglas was still in school, he was deeply impacted by something his football coach said one time during training. Timmy explained:

> *The coach looked at all the freshmen who were about to start off-season and said, 'When it gets hard during this next couple of months, look at the person next to you. If they're doing it, you can do it too.'*

Timmy took this to heart and that mindset first got him through his football season and then into his adult life. Timmy now says to himself, 'Look at the person next to me. If they're doing it I can do it too.' In fact, he told us he has extrapolated the person next to him to anybody on the planet or who has ever lived. The guidance Timmy received from his mentor at the age of 14 has now morphed into 'If a human can do it, I can do it too'.

Maryam Mohiuddin Ahmed told us about her spiritual mentor, a man very learned and wise in Islamic Sufi philosophy. Maryam went to him because she felt lost and was unsure of where she was going and what she was meant to be doing. Her mentor asked her, 'Well, where are you right now? Because if you don't know where you are, how are you going to know where you have to go?' Maryam's mentor helped her take a step back and discover who she really was and where she was right now. In doing that, Maryam explained, 'more and more doors kept opening'.

So far, we've talked about how the people in our guests' lives became their role models, but we were intrigued to discover that not everyone looks to other humans for a role model. In fact, we were delighted to learn that nature herself could provide us with the ultimate role model!

Nature: the most perfect role model of all

It was Amaranatho who first pointed out to us that nature is a much better role model than humans. He acknowledges that, while there are plenty of wise people out there, in the end, we and our connection to the universe are the best role models. He said a role model could be a tree, the sky or nature itself because it's always teaching us, and that the problem with the role model approach is that it is based on the hero/heroine model, which is no longer serving us. The model that needs to be built up now is that of community, collaboration and supporting one another.

Julie Trager says we don't actually need anything outside of ourselves and that, even though humans are far from perfect, 'we all have exactly what we need to move forward on our path without any outside influences'. Julie says nature is a perfect reflection of God and serves to remind us that we are connected to everything. As she so eloquently puts it:

> Bees and hawks and trees and flowers and grass, they all just do what they're meant to do naturally because it's hardwired into them – that connection, or interconnection, with everything else. There's so little efforting involved with nature. It just does what it's meant to do. And I honestly think that as humans, if we started to live more like that, we'd be much happier creatures and the world would be more peaceful, quite frankly.

A final note on role models

People who do audacious things tend to become role models for others, or at least become inspirational, if not aspirational. When we tap into our own inner wisdom, we realise that we know more than we give ourselves credit for. Our inner wisdom, hinted at above by Amaranatho and Julie, and also referred to as *the inner mentor* or *the sage*, represents a more evolved, wiser version of ourselves that already has the answers to our dilemmas and questions. In other words, our own personal role model.

Terry Tucker talks about four types of people in the world: common and ordinary people, who are the vast majority; motivational people, who are usually looking for some kind of personal reward for helping others; inspirational people, who inspire us to be better in our lives; and aspirational people, who we aspire to be like. Terry believes we were all born to be uncommon and extraordinary and, in living such lives, we can be that inspirational, or even aspirational, role model for both ourselves and others.

And that inspiration must come from education and encouragement, not force or regulation, according to Gavin Scott. Gavin says the only way to raise people's awareness and levels of consciousness is to be a beacon of hope ourselves, to be the light that shines inspiration everywhere from a place of kindness and no judgement. Gavin signs off his emails with 'If you can choose to be anything in life, choose to be inspirational'. What a wonderful vision to have!

Nature is by far the role model that touched us and stayed in our hearts. Nature offers herself up as an inspiration of what it means to be our true and authentic selves, showing us we can be non-judgemental and in full acceptance of our surroundings. Indeed what, other than nature, is as magnificent in her beauty and perfection? She will always live and develop to her fullest potential. That has to be the biggest inspiration of them all!

Questions for the reader to consider

If you **have already done** something audacious, who or what helped you in the pursuit of your audacious goal? What did you learn from them?

If you **would like to do** something audacious, are there people who can help you in the pursuit of your audacious goal? If not, how can you find them? Do you even feel you need role models?

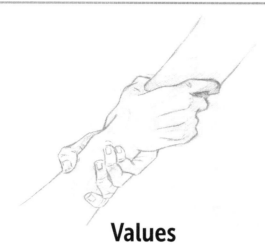

Chapter Eight

Values

V alues can be simply described as things that are especially important to us; for example, family, health, security, freedom. They are the theme of our lives, perpetually present with us and in us, although we may not always be aware of them. They have led us to where we are today, shaping us as individual human beings and determining how we perceive the world and how we are perceived by others. Someone who values their personal health, for instance, will attach great importance to diet, exercise and lifestyle. Thanks to their systematic efforts, they are likely to enjoy vitality and will be perceived by others as an example of good health.

We can also interpret values as goals that we want to achieve in the long run, goals that may change over time depending on our current stage of life. The values that are attractive to young people just entering adulthood will be different to those of people developing their careers and starting their own families, and very different from those of people who have raised children and are coming to the end of their professional careers.

Terry Tucker says it's important to tie our goals to our values. He says too many people set goals that are 'just floating out there' because they are not tied to our personal principles or morals. Terry challenges us to ask the question, what are you willing to die for? By doing that we are giving our goals a foundation, meaning they'll be much easier to achieve than if we were to 'just throw them out there not attached to anything'.

Dalia Feldheim says one way of identifying our values is to map our lives and examine the points where we experienced highs and lows. She says in many cases the pain points show us what our values are and what we really care about, and if we're witnessing pain in either ourselves or in others, that's a very strong motivator to take action. We touched on some of these pain points in Chapter One when we discussed triggers.

When we asked our guests about their values, we found that the goals they set themselves were very much aligned with what they believed in. Most of those values were about being of service to others, but some guests also talked about caring for the planet and some about living without fear. Let's look at some examples of how we can, in Terry Tucker's words, tie our goals to our values.

Being of service to others

Living a life of service is the most fulfilling and rewarding life that one can lead, says Gavin Scott, a view shared by Maryam Mohiuddin Ahmed, who told us about the concept of Ubuntu – 'I am because you are' or, in other words, 'There is no I if there is no You'. And Ousmane Pame spoke of a saying in the Wolof language that translates as 'one person is another person's medicine'.

Ousmane asserts that if we want to find out who we are then we need to be at the service of other people. Maryam says when we think of our higher purpose, of why we are here, it is for each other and we must, therefore, learn how to serve each other. In that service is how we will find ourselves, where we are and where we ought to go.

Being of service to others is about aligning our values, beliefs and higher purpose to our actions, behaviours and goals. This is precisely what Cecilia Chiolerio did when she launched a startup offering people collaborative workspaces in cafés and restaurants that were otherwise empty during the day. Cecilia explains how her business aligns with her values:

> I really have this issue when I see people lonely and I always try to do something to help them out. Loneliness in the workplace is something that's not spoken about and, when we're talking about freelancers or, in my case, a startup founder, you can really feel alone. And you're alone in the worst moment ever because you're creating your business and that's hard, so it's really important to have people around you. That's what makes me wake up in the morning – I see that I'm doing good for someone else. And that fits with what I believe in.

Claire Tonna also spoke about loneliness, telling us she writes and performs songs that help her feel a sense of belonging in 'this pretty much lonely world'. Like Maryam, Claire views humanity as one big family that needs to help each other and she says what makes her happy is the service she provides to others in contributing to their joy and peace.

Nik Pandya places immense value on the need for children to develop important life skills such as building resilience, handling relationships and dealing with disappointment. This is what compelled Nik to start working on projects that nurture children's intra- and interpersonal skills and to help them and their families lead meaningful lives in modern society.

Being of service to the community was the driving force behind Kenneth Mackay's long struggle for a road to connect his remote village with the rest of the island. Kenneth talked of the hardship of having to seek medical attention for members of the community by making the arduous journey over a mountainous track in all weathers and often in the middle of the night. It was on one of these trips that Kenneth's uncle had a heart attack and perished on the mountain. Terry Tucker advised us that in order to give our goals a foundation we should ask the question 'what are you willing to die for?' We can safely say that Kenneth's goal was built on an exceptionally solid foundation, with one family member already having died for it.

Jessa de la Morena has made it her mission to help others discover, or *un*cover, their own inner hero. Jessa's cancer diagnosis forced her to stop and evaluate what was important for her and she found that most of what we do and think in our daily lives is, in fact, automatic. Jessa said that once we start observing our actions we can make the conscious choice to either continue doing them or question whether they are still serving our current beliefs and values. Jessa's condition led her to not only start her community U Are The Hero, but to also become a transformational coach in order to help others transform their lives.

When Lynn Yap couldn't be at her grandmother's side during her final days, it left her with a level of guilt and shame that caused her to reassess her values. Lynn asked herself what she wanted to invest her time in, who she wanted to spend her time with and how she wanted to be of service to others and give value to the community. Lynn decided to leave her banking career and do voluntary work mentoring entrepreneurs, especially women, ultimately setting up a network to support young women and girls.

With similar values to Lynn, Felicia Specht also started a networking organisation to help young women. Felicia told us:

> *Girls are still limiting their dreams a lot and that's what I'm working for. It was my absolute goal to be part of the movement to help young women follow their goals and dreams and not see obstacles or barriers, not to think in genders, not to even think 'maybe this is*

not the right thing for me because I'm a girl.

Eliminating that thought from young girls' minds is what drives Felicia to do what she does.

Dalia Feldheim's values also centre around empowering women. Dalia has converted those values into action, first in her corporate job marketing feminine hygiene products and later in her independent consultancy work, which aims to help women be the best they can be and achieve their full potential.

And Omolade Femi-Ajao, who is working to improve access for ethnic minority women to health, social and community services in the UK, says her vision is to love her neighbour as she loves herself. What drives Omolade is her belief that everyone should be able to 'achieve whatever it is they want to achieve' and to 'give people the skill sets and the tools they need to be able to do that'.

For Alistair Maigurira and Peter Guess, their guiding principle is the impact they can have on society. Peter says he is aware of the difficulties people are facing every day and this is why he became a social activist in the first place. Alistair told us he took the time to articulate the vision, mission and values of their diversity and inclusion consultancy practice, which is ultimately to create an inclusive world. He came to the conclusion that it's critical to do the work now and lay the foundations for the next generation to build on, so that in the future an inclusive world *will* be possible.

Jen Armstrong has a very inclusive vision of the future, where oppression and captivity no longer exist and love and freedom are the norm. For us to get there, Jen says, we all need to be our authentic, higher selves:

> *I don't think a happy, content person wants to hurt another person and I don't think a happy, content person wants to hurt another animal. So in a world where we're all living in our higher selves, animals will be free. And if animals are free, we're free – free to be joyful and*

free to be experiencing life.

Jen has translated her values into composing and performing songs which raise awareness of the rights of all to a life of freedom from oppression.

Presumably sharing similar values is Judy Boyle, who founded an organisation that raises awareness about human trafficking. Judy experienced a pain point in her life when she first found out about this heinous crime and was driven to act on her values to be of service to those who were suffering because of it. Judy said, 'You may choose to look the other way, but you can no longer say you do not know.' That has been the driving force that has led her to campaign for human freedom from oppression for more than 20 years.

Timmy Douglas felt a pain point at a young age when he realised how widespread poverty is and the suffering it causes, and he has set himself the audacious goal of finding a way to alleviate world poverty. Timmy says he feels morally obligated to help people in pain.

Mark Matamisa's pain point happened when he visited his home country of Zimbabwe and discovered that people were dying due to a lack of access to safe drinking water. Mark believes that everyone has a right to clean water and he put those beliefs into action by founding an initiative to bring clean water to the people who need it most, responding to a moral obligation to serve those in dire need.

Debbie Levitt also feels morally obligated to be of service to others. She does this by making her work available for free or at very low cost, as she feels everyone should have access to what she's producing, regardless of their economic background. Debbie told us she has published hundreds of hours of content online, and when she was asked why she doesn't start a school, she replied:

> *As soon as I charge for it, there goes a whole bunch of people who should be in that school. I can't make that model work, because that 'save the world' person inside of me says this should be free for the people.*

Returning to Jen's call for authenticity, this is a value shared by Tish Joyce. Tish made the most of the time she spent running across Europe alone to reflect on her values, and said she found the clarity and balance she needed to be able to achieve what she wanted in her life, which is to be authentic. Formerly, Tish would try to conform to other people's expectations of her but now she realises that being her own authentic self is the most important thing. As a result, Tish is happy and content and is loving life. And it is from this place of authenticity, contentment and love for life that Tish is able to help others in her new line of work as a natural healer.

It was honouring her own authenticity that led Julie Trager to become a spiritual mentor for others. Julie told us she had experienced misery and burnout in her former career because she had been living for so long in a 'narrow little box that society had prescribed for me'. Julie surrendered to God, which changed her life completely, and since then she has dedicated herself to

> helping other people find those aspects of themselves that have been locked away in tiny little boxes, and open them up to their own authenticity, their own intuition, their own sense of purpose and mission and to help them walk into that.

To Julie, that's what living life as a fierce life-warrior is all about.

This same topic of authenticity, or the lack of it, is a recurring trope in Maribel's adult life. Personal development and doing work that is fulfilling are two of her core values, and that is why working with people who wish to learn how to be more assertive, be more disagreeable and stand up for themselves creates alignment in her life and gives her a grounded purpose. She wants to support people in achieving their potential and creating such a solid sense of self that criticism or the opinions of others do not matter. It's a way of achieving personal freedom and autonomy.

Caring for our planet

Ousmane Pame has dedicated his life's work to reviving the Sahel in West Africa. Ousmane works with local communities to encourage them to appreciate the value of caring for our planet, the local environment and the people around them. He is aiming to reinvent what friendship is, what fraternity across borders is, and what it means to live a safe, peaceful and productive life. He wishes to help communities understand the necessity of trying to preserve their natural resources and he has faith that, although we're still growing together as humans, one day we'll get there. Ousmane told us:

> We're on a journey and we're facing so many challenges. Our children, though they may have bigger ecological challenges, have bigger chances to connect with other youth in the world so that they can also live together in much better conditions than we do today. So, there is hope and, although it's just a flame in the wind, it's resisting and there will be more candles around, and then people can really start thinking about how to reinvent our fraternity and live like brothers and sisters all around the world.

Farhana Yamin has used her professional background as a lawyer to work for the benefit of the planet and all who live on it. Farhana strongly values environmental justice, especially for less industrialised and more vulnerable countries, working at an international level on treaties which 'hold governments and big polluters to account'. Her values on this are so strong that she even glued herself to the building of an oil company in protest. She also helped set up a project in her local community which brings people together to work on solutions for social and environmental issues.

Gavin Scott told us his values in terms of environment and sustainability go back a long way. In his former position as founder of a luxury residential development company, he said he would use eco-friendly materials and sustainable processes wherever possible. Gavin feels we are coming very close to the point of no return for our planet unless we take pride in caring for our environment. He would like to see everyone start making small changes in their lives as the overall impact would be great, but he acknowledges that change must start from within. In 2022, Gavin set himself the audacious goal of swimming the English Channel to raise awareness around plastic pollution in the oceans, an issue he feels passionate about.

Rika Cossey is also concerned about the state of our planet and is taking steps to prepare her young family for what might come by embarking on a life of self-sufficiency. Rika told us she is raising their own meat and growing their own vegetables – with all the challenges that entails – as this is essential to their mission of providing security for her family's future. Although Rika doesn't like to talk about doom and gloom, she's aware of the need to be prepared for emergencies such as power outages or empty grocery stores. Rika says we don't know if societies are going to collapse and she questions what will happen if they do, saying if we build our systems on sandy ground, what happens when the sand gives way? Rika tries to counter her worries about the future by trying to prepare her family for being self-sufficient, and to not have to rely on a system that might or might not get us through.

Helen can totally relate to the values described by Rika, Gavin and Ousmane. You may recall that Helen's primary motive for moving to a remote location was to become self-sufficient in the production of her own food and energy. Her aim is to provide inspiration for her B&B guests of an alternative way of life than the one we've been conditioned by society into accepting, and she has discovered that one of the things she values the most is living in peace and harmony with our beautiful planet. The other thing she identified as being very important to her is personal freedom, which is connected to the final value that came up during the audacious conversations we had with our guests.

Living without fear

Philip Keay equates being free of fear to having self-control over our emotions and, therefore, our reactions to external situations, since that level of self-control serves as our guide. Philip says if we're living by our own guide – our own Ten Commandments, so to speak – then we're living by values rather than fear. Our values are the personal ones that we've chosen to fit us, and if we live according to those chosen values then there is no room for fear in our lives, and this allows us to do the audacious things the world needs.

Intrepid traveller Susanne Hillmer gave us an example of how she has learned to live without fear. Susanne told us she thrives on challenges and on pushing the boundaries of her comfort zone because it gives her confirmation that there's nothing in life she can't handle. Susanne says putting herself in novel, non-routine situations while travelling makes her feel vibrant, and whenever a problem arises she can stay calm and focused and come up with a non-fear-based solution. She has learned to free herself from fear and this gives her an immense feeling of liberty and gratitude, or as Susanne puts it, 'I like to feel myself being alive'.

At the same time that Tish Joyce discovered the value of living an authentic life, she found she was suddenly free of fear. Tish told us she'd always been seeking things outside of herself to make her happy, until it dawned on her: 'It was all inside me and I could be happy if I just accepted me and realised in this minute, I'm okay. I'm good enough.' Tish says that it's a very simple thing to do and that

it's not about going off meditating, it's literally just being present in this moment and accepting yourself. And once you can do that life is really easy.

When we spoke with Terry Tucker, he told us very candidly, 'In all honesty, I'm more than likely coming to the end of my life.' Terry has been battling a rare form of cancer for ten years and has come to the conclusion that 'dying is not nearly as scary if you find the reason you were put on the face of this earth and you live it'. In truth, we're all going to die but, as Terry says, 'not every one of us is going to really live'. He quoted a Native American proverb that says:

When you are born, you cry and the world rejoices. Live your life in such a way so that when you die, the world cries and you rejoice.

In other words, if we live our lives according to our values and purpose in life, then death is nothing to fear at all. Realising this grants us the permission to really live.

Our values guide us in our growth and development. When we are able to connect the dots, creating an existence that is authentically aligned with our personal values, life makes much more sense. And when we strive to live as much in harmony with our values as possible, then the reward will be a sense of inner consistency, satisfaction and contentment with our lives.

Questions for the reader to consider

If you **have already done** something audacious, describe how the audacious thing you did aligns with your values.

If you **would like to do** something audacious, describe how the audacious thing you want to do aligns with your values.

Chapter Nine

Advice

We asked our guests what advice they would give to anyone wishing to pursue an audacious goal and we received some wonderful insights and perspectives on what people find important for living an audacious life.

These ranged from personal aspects such as finding our purpose, slowing down and taking care of ourselves, to interpersonal aspects such as involving others in our goals and learning from those who went before us, to very practical aspects such as simply making a start on whatever it is we wish to achieve and never giving up.

Let's find out what our guests had to say on these points.

Personal Aspects

Find your purpose and do what feels right

Maryam Mohiuddin Ahmed gives excellent advice on how to find our purpose. She says we should first discover who we are in relation to the land, to people and to our feelings, and then observe which patterns emerge. This will lead us to uncover what kind of person we are at heart and what we are attracting. And the good thing is, all this knowledge and wisdom is already within us. We can read all the books we want and search outside for information but, ultimately, the universe is inside all of us. Once we see that, we start seeing unity with everything else; we see patterns emerge and then we know what to do because

> opportunities suddenly show up, people suddenly show up and something inside you goes, 'Oh, this is what I was waiting for. This is who I needed to meet. This is the conversation I needed to have. Now I know what to do.' So the minute you give space to it, it emerges, that's how you know. But understand, the more you go inside, the more the world will pull you out. And that is when you know you're on the right track.

Jessa de la Morena also went inside herself to find that wisdom. When considering the myriad ways the doctors were proposing for treating her cancer, Jessa had to take measures to find out what was the right thing to do. We can make lists and debate and be as analytical as we want about things, but what Jessa did, after gathering the relevant information, was to sit quietly with herself and ask how she really felt about each option. It was through this stilling of her mind that the answer would appear. Jessa explains:

> It rests upon you to make a decision about what you're going to do and the only way to know that answer is to sit with yourself and feel inside what feels right to you. I used to be very analytical and would debate things with my friends and list the pros and cons and I don't do any of that anymore. It's just tiring. I inform myself, I interview people who have more resources than I do about certain information. And then I take it back, and I just sit with it, and I say 'Okay, what feels right to me?' And that's where you're aligning that

decision with your values and your core essence.

Terry Tucker advises us to control our mind, otherwise our mind will control us, and one way of doing this is through meditation. Tish Joyce found that running the equivalent of a marathon a day was a form of meditation for her. Tish advises that whatever we wish to do, we should just do it and enjoy it without getting caught up in trying to prove things to ourselves or others.

Likewise, Dalia Feldheim advises us not to wait to do what we love. Life is short and we should bring what we love into the here and now and just do it, focusing on what we *can* do rather than what we can't. Dalia uses a very fitting analogy of a sailing boat. She explains:

> *Our strengths are our sail. If it's not up, we won't be able to move forward. Our weaknesses are the holes that we have in the sail. Should we close those holes? Yes. But if we close the holes and the sail is not up, will we move forward? No. So the idea is to put your sail up and do whatever you need to neutralise those weaknesses, to close those holes. But really, most of the time we need to focus on our strengths.*

Slow down

Angela Papalia really learned to slow down when she relocated from a busy law firm in Canada to an online practice in rural Mexico. She still did the same amount of work, but on her own terms. Angela relayed the story of a colleague who would get upset when clients would email late at night. Angela's advice to her colleague?

> *Just because that's when they're asking you doesn't mean that's when you have to answer. Just let it go. The input doesn't have to dictate the output, especially in terms of timing. So let them ask the question and you answer it when you answer it, reasonably.*

Angela told us it feels quite scary to say that now, as she used to be that person herself, feeling she had to deal with her emails right away for fear of missing them or forgetting them or allowing her inbox to fill up and become overwhelming. Now she's slowed right down, but says, 'I'm still as productive. I'm not sure how, but I am.'

Nik Pandya says that our greatest commodity is time, not money. If we lose money, we can earn it back, but we can't earn back time. Once we've lost it, it's gone. And when we start thinking of time as our greatest commodity, then we'll slow down and respect it more.

Debbie Levitt also recommends slowing down. One way she did this was to change her physical environment by relocating from the US to a small community on the island of Sardinia, and switching her mindset to 'island time', since 'there's only so long your American or London or Berlin mindset is going to work for you in a community on island time'.

Debbie says it took her two years of living there to stop eating at her desk while working, which was what she'd been used to in America. She now takes long, slow lunches and connects with the community more. Debbie says, 'We are our environments and it's very hard to change yourself when you're still in that same environment.'

By changing our environment, we change the way we interact with and serve our fellow humans. Debbie laments the way 'we're in such a global rush to give people crap'. She says we should slow down and give them something better and that this works for everything, including lunches and relationships, and that when we get over-obsessed with time and money we end up worshipping the wrong idols and having the wrong priorities.

The environment plays a key role for Tish Joyce, who also made the decision to move to a place which encouraged slow living. Tish told us:

> *I'm grateful every day because I live in a beautiful place, I have lovely people around me, and I feel like I'm part of the community. And I*

think that's because I've slowed right down and connected with so many people. I've found my dharma, my reason for being.

Take care of yourself

By far the most popular piece of advice our guests gave was the importance of taking care of ourselves, be it physically, mentally, emotionally or spiritually. Indeed, one of our guests learned this the hard way.

Andrea Heuston, who almost died on the operating table and spent the following eight months in recovery, says:

I'm very careful about my health because I never want to be in a position again where I don't have it. Because your health really is everything. Without your health, you can't do anything else.

Andrea is now mindful of what she eats, and she's made it a part of her routine to walk four miles every morning before starting her work and ten miles over the course of each day.

Myah Payel Mitra has realised in her work as a movement therapy practitioner that women often put the needs and cares of others first, while forgetting to take care of themselves. She encourages bringing that back into our consciousness and making self-care a daily ritual and, in fact, the centre of our lives.

So, how can we make self-care a daily part of our lives? This is what yoga therapist Vicky Arundel's work is all about. She offers some invaluable advice on this topic, recommending we set ourselves boundaries and continually learn new things to avoid burnout, 'so that when you show up to work, you can be the best that you can possibly be'.

For Vicky that means going on long walks, cooking a new recipe or getting lost in an engrossing book to keep her mind active. She also takes the time to plan her days, saying, 'The success of the next day really depends on the planning the night before.' Vicky says that getting into the practice of planning your days the evening before forces you to 'first of all think about how much time you have, and secondly, what are the priorities, what are the most important things?' And above all, to ask yourself if the tasks you're setting for the next day fit in with your values. Vicky goes on to say:

> Anybody who has their own business, you're looking at a long-haul project here. This is a marathon, not a sprint, and burnout is a thing. I've definitely gone through periods of it. And I've seen many people who also run their own businesses who have really struggled with periods of burnout. So, self-care practices and setting boundaries are critical if you're going to go forwards for the long term. You've got to have systems set up in place."

Charlene Camilleri Duca told us that if she doesn't do at least 30 minutes of yoga or meditation four times a week, she feels a difference in her mood and in her ability to be grateful. Charlene recognises the importance of allowing time for physical exercise, meditation and being alone.

Angela Papalia reaped the benefits of taking care of herself almost as soon as she moved to Mexico. She told us:

> I'm very rarely stressed now. I sleep like a baby, which I didn't before. If I woke up at any point in the middle of the night, it would take hours to get back to sleep. And that's not the case anymore. And it happened almost instantly after I got here.

Colin O'Donohoe reminds us that we're only human and that we should take care of our basic needs of physical, mental, emotional and spiritual nourishment. He says:

> You have to remember that you're human. You have to remember to rest. You have to remember to nourish yourself. And that's why I also do my own personal solo projects. I compose my own music for myself, I

do a lot of performing on Native American flutes and drums that feed my soul. I'm not doing it to be a star, I'm not doing it for attention, I'm doing it purely for selfish reasons to make myself feel good.

It's not selfish to take care of yourself. In fact, it's self*less*. Tish Joyce had a hard time learning to love herself, often beating herself up about not achieving her running goals, until she realised she was more likely to perform better if she accepted that sometimes there are 'bad' days. Now her advice to anyone is to love and be gentle on themself.

Lynn Yap gives similar advice. She says:

Develop patience and kindness for yourself. Patience is a really big one. Sometimes things don't go fast enough when you're trying to build your own organisation. And I'm learning to be kinder because there's so much to learn and do. And it's okay, as long as I'm moving in the same direction. That's what I tell myself – as long as I keep going in the direction that I'm heading, that's all that matters.

Timmy Douglas says we need to show up for ourselves and do what gives us energy. Although Timmy's audacious goal is to end world poverty, he says real wealth is in our energy levels, our health levels and the health of our relationships. He told us:

You have people who are dead broke and a lot happier than I am and that's because they figured out those other parts of life. Just because you're financially free does not mean you're free. Make sure you don't forget about that.

Dalia Feldheim concurs, saying it's not about managing time, it's about managing energy. In her previous job, although she 'worked like crazy', she was 'on fire', but was nevertheless able to recognise when she needed to take a digital detox. Dalia says stress is not a bad thing per se, as it helps us to focus and increases our mental capacity, but the problem is not stress, it's lack of recovery. We can't expect to operate at 100% every day without time to recover, which includes getting plenty of sleep and eating wholesome food.

Watching what we eat and drink is something Mike Patterson has been researching in great detail over the years. Mike told us that our bodies are slightly alkaline[1] and that if we keep our body in this state, we are less likely to get sick. He says we should avoid acidic substances, such as coffee and carbonated drinks, opting instead for pure water (which, naturally, has not been chemically treated).

Let go of attachments

They say travel opens the mind. What it also does is highlight the extent of the trappings we tend to accumulate when we stay in one place. This is something Helen discovered on the various trips she did with her motorcycle or campervan, and it's also what some of our guests experienced on their travels.

When Tish Joyce was running across Europe with everything she needed in a backpack, including her tent, she realised how heavy the baggage she'd left behind really was. Tish told us about her 'gorgeous house, great job, nice lifestyle, international career and financial independence', but on her seven-week run, she had none of that. She said:

> I carried nothing with me. I didn't need any of those things. And when I got back I felt healthier than I'd ever felt in my life. I got back to my six-bedroom home and said, 'What is this?' I couldn't understand why I had so much stuff. I went into the bathroom cupboard and said, 'What is all this stuff?' The day I came home, within 24 hours I took so many boxes to charity. And I knew then that I needed

1 | It is 7.365 on the 1–14 pH scale www.getoffyouracid.com/blogs/ph-info/7-365-the-ph-secret-to-health-energy

to sell my house because it was too big. I didn't need it anymore. The children had grown up and it was just excessive. It was gorgeous. I'd spent all my time creating this lovely home, but it was not what I needed. I needed something far less than that.

Charlene Camilleri Duca came to a similar conclusion when she was travelling around Europe with her young family, staying in rented accommodation while continuing her psychology practice remotely. As she approached the end of her trip, she told us, 'I think we could get rid of half of the things that we have now, because if I haven't used something for the last two weeks, then it means that I don't need it.'

Charlene explained that people are very good at adapting and getting by with less, and that comfort is not always a good thing. She said that when we get used to being comfortable, we're constantly wishing we had more comforts, which actually makes us feel worse. For example, at home she thought that in order to work she needed a good desk, a good chair and air conditioning. Now she realises she can do most things without having the 'necessary' comforts we think we must have. Ultimately, we need to let go of anything that is not serving us.

Interpersonal Aspects
Involve others

For many of our guests, it's the sharing of our goals with others that makes an endeavour worthwhile. For example, Cecilia Chiolerio says:

Find the right people – for a tough job, for a sport challenge, whatever. You need the right people beside you, otherwise it's not much fun when you achieve your goals and you're there alone.

For Jen Taylor, involving others serves another purpose. Jen says that if we tell our friends and family *what* we intend to do before we've sorted out *how* we're going to do it, then this helps avoid procrastination. She explains:

> Once you've clarified what your goal is, then leave the practicalities and the organisational things till after that, rather than making up your mind after you've thought about the practicalities, because you could go round and round in circles. It opens up the doors if you just let things evolve after you've made the decision.

Colin O'Donohoe emphasises how important it is to involve and really listen to others from a place of humility. His advice is:

> The number one thing you can do is listen to the people you want to work with. Take a back seat, humble yourself, have the self-confidence that you already know you're good, but you don't have to show it every day, every minute. Show respect, do the research, don't make the focus on yourself. And then others want to learn more about you, but only because you first shut up and let them tell you about them.

Likewise, Lynn Yap appreciates that involving others can be beneficial to achieving our audacious goals, as it helps us develop perseverance and grit. She says that, although it's easy to develop passion for a particular subject or topic, perseverance is something that we have to learn, and that if we get others to support us in our journeys, learning from them and seeing how they have done it, we can increase our perseverance and grit in whatever goals we would like to achieve. She gives the example of preparing for a race:

> Let's say you're preparing for a marathon on your own. It helps if you train and work out with someone else; that will help you persevere through that marathon, through the gruelling preparation in the run-up to that race. But even during the marathon, imagine your network of supporters that really helps you persevere to the finish line.

Learn from those who went before us

As Lynn says, we can increase our own perseverance by learning from those who went before us, and this is a piece of advice that many of our guests gave.

Omolade Femi-Ajao says we shouldn't be afraid to ask for help, and in turn, we will be the ones helping those who come after us. Omolade believes we should ride on the shoulders of giants and learn from people who have gone ahead of us so that we don't have to go through the same stresses. Omolade told us:

> I learned early on to ask for help. It is not a sign of weakness to ask for charity. If you need help, you ask for it. And people are going to give you help and then, of course, you are able to help other people as well.

Recognising our own vulnerabilities and not being afraid to ask for help is part of life and, as Omolade says, we will be the ones, in turn, helping others. Terry Tucker puts it beautifully when he says, 'What you leave behind is what you weave in the hearts of other people.'

Jen Taylor would agree with Omolade. When she was planning her campervan trip with her family, she contacted people who had undertaken similar voyages. Jen says we tend to assume that no one has done what we want to do, but that's rarely true and if we find just one role model, then our own goals seem less scary, especially if the other person is willing to share their insights with us to avoid us making obvious mistakes.

Helen can vouch for this advice, as she really benefited from reading Anne Cholawo's book *Island on the Edge* when she was making the decision to move to a remote location in the Outer Hebrides. She thought, 'Well if this lady can move to a small island with even fewer resources than where I intend to go, then I can certainly do it.'

Felicia Specht advises following in the footsteps of those whose journey is similar to the one we wish to take. She says it's important to

draw inspiration and listen to advice from people whose path you would love to follow. There's no point listening to advice that comes from a person living a totally different life than what I am looking for right now.

Maryam Mohiuddin Ahmed not only recommends following others who have gone before but teaming up with others who are on the same path now. She says that when we're trying to do something audacious, we should take comfort in the fact that we're not alone and that there's a whole tribe of people out there just like us who are probably as scared as we are. And then when we find these people,

for starters, you could be scared together. And then you could think, if we weren't scared, what could we do together? And then you could plan together and conspire together and eventually change yourselves together. And in that changing of yourselves, you may actually change some part of the world.

Practical Aspects
Make a start

Finally, some of our guests offered the advice that, if we wish to achieve our audacious goals, then at some point we need to make a start on them. There are different viewpoints about how much research and forward planning we should do in advance, but ultimately, we're not going to achieve anything unless we simply make a start.

Anne Cholawo told us how she planned in advance for her move to a small Scottish island. The way she did it was to sit down and write 'for' and 'against' on a piece of paper and list on one side all the reasons she wanted to do it and on the other side all the things that could go wrong. She advises being brutally honest with ourselves, taking care not to overestimate our capabilities, but also not underestimating ourselves either. Anne told us:

> *[Although it's tempting to say] 'I'll never be able to do that', you just don't know until you try. Just face everything face on, the best of it and the worst of it. And if you still want to do it, if you can see the downsides to it, then go for it.*

Mark Matamisa also advocates doing the research and then just going for it. When launching a new product, Mark says that 'putting something out there that's good is magnitudes better than launching a perfect product years down the road' because no manner of modelling or desk-based research can give us the insights we can learn from customer feedback, which then feeds into refinements and further innovations.

However, Mark cautions:

> *bravado will never replace the hard work of market research and product development and strategy development. Because if you don't have a sound base, your entrepreneurial journey is going to be short. It doesn't matter how brilliant it starts, it will be short, in spite of you having started.*

Aurora Pérez-Vico says it's never the perfect time to start as there will always be disruptions, but we should stop using that as an excuse for procrastination and instead just go for it. Aurora advocates not being afraid to go out of our comfort zone and developing a positive mindset that says yes to exploring new paths.

We'll end this section with a classic piece of advice offered by Jen Taylor:

> *The best way to get something done is to begin.*

Break things down

When our audacious goal seems overwhelming and too large to handle, one way of dealing with this is to break things down. Nik Pandya recommends doing one small thing each day that pushes the project or moves us towards our goal, and we'll be amazed at what we can achieve in a month. If that then becomes a habit, we suddenly become very productive without actually trying.

Omolade Femi-Ajao offers similar advice. She told us that big goals are made up of small goals and she just focuses on the tiny 200 feet in front of her. For Omolade that means publishing a paper or doing a small study to generate evidence to advance her research project. She's happy with every small step she's able to take.

Tish Joyce told us that she's always taken things step by step in her life. Just like managing a project at work, when she was preparing to run across Europe she thought, 'Okay, what's the first step? I need to figure out a route. What's the second step? I need to figure out what I'm going to carry.' Tish says breaking everything down into solvable chunks is just like life.

Prepare well

When we spoke with Gavin Scott, he was preparing to swim the English Channel to raise awareness around plastic pollution in the oceans. We asked Gavin for a piece of advice about his goal and he said, 'The better you prepare for something, the easier your challenge will go.'

Never give up

One final and very important piece of advice from our guests is to never give up on your goals. When we asked Scottish islander

Kenneth Mackay for advice for others pursuing audacious goals, he replied, 'Keep at it! If there's a battle that's worth anything, it's a battle just to keep at it.'

Terry Tucker expressed a similar sentiment. He told us:

> *As long as you don't quit, you can never be defeated. Embrace the pain and the difficulty that we all experience in life and use that pain and difficulty to make you a stronger and more resilient individual.*

We're very grateful for the advice and everything else that our audacious guests offered. We have learned so much from their personal journeys and from the experiences they shared with us, and it has brought both Maribel and Helen far in their own life journeys. We're coming now to one of our favourite points in the conversations with our guests, which is when we ask the final question about what gives them the solid grounding to continue with their goals, despite everything life is throwing at them. Let's find out how they responded to this important question.

Questions for the reader to consider

If you **have already done** something audacious, what advice would you give to your younger self who is just starting out on this audacious journey?

If you **would like to do** something audacious, take a moment to imagine you have already done it. Ask your future self to give you some advice on making a start on your audacious journey. Where is your future self now? What does their life look like?

Chapter Ten

Solid Grounding

Be like the promontory against which the waves continually break,
but it stands firm and tames the fury of the water around it.
                                               — Marcus Aurelius (Meditations 4:49)

A t the end of each interview our guests are given the opportunity to share what it is that gives them the solid grounding to pursue their audacious goal. This is the ultimate question we ask all our guests:

> *The name of our podcast is AudaciousNess. The 'audacious' part*
> *relates to having the audacity to set yourself such a goal in the first*
> *place. The word 'ness' is an archaic term for a spit of land which juts*
> *out into the sea; in other words, solid ground surrounded by the*
> *constant and, at times, tumultuous motion of wind and water. So,*
> *for us, AudaciousNess means having a solid grounding on which to*
> *practise your audacity. Our final question to you is, while you were*
> *pursuing your goal, where did you get the solid grounding to continue*

while everything else was in motion? How did you stay grounded in your vision, despite what life was throwing at you?

We received a range of responses to this question but, as with much of the content of this book, common threads appeared throughout those responses. We have grouped the responses into six broad categories and we'll let each guest speak for themselves:

A deep belief and certainty in what I'm doing

A deep faith and belief that what I'm doing has value. I just truly believe in [what I'm doing]. —*Vicky Arundel*

I want to make the world a better place, and if you believe in what you're doing, you don't care about what people are saying. I'm going to use my energy to stick to my purpose and to my vision and do my thing, no matter what happens around me. —*Nahia Orduña*

An inner certainty that what you're doing is the right thing. If you're not certain what you're doing, if you're two-minded about anything you're doing, you're going to have the element of giving up. But if you're absolutely certain you're on the right road, on doing the right thing, and it's what you want, there's no two minds about it. That's what makes you stand. —*Anne Cholawo*

What keeps me grounded is focusing on my purpose, my essence, why I'm here, why I'm doing what I'm doing. And I'm doing it because I firmly believe that I don't want others to feel alone like I did. That's my passion that drives me forward. —*Jessa de la Morena*

Having an idea of where I want to go. When so many things are thrown your way, and there are going to be things, it can be challenging at times to carry on with your goal. —*Katie Taylor*

The foundation of everything is our values. Whatever I do, I'm always trying to help people. These are the foundations and I know what I want and why I want it. I have a certain amount of knowledge that, if I don't share it, in the not-too-distant future it's going to be lost. —*Mike Patterson*

My spiritual beliefs and practices

Faith has been a huge part of what's kept me grounded. It's a constant circular journey and there have been moments where I've questioned everything. But that constant struggle and that circular dance is what keeps me grounded; knowing that even if I've hit the end, I'm going to hit the start again soon. —*Maryam Mohiuddin Ahmed*

Faith in humanity and that we're still growing together as humans. Hope is here; it's a flame in the wind, but it's resisting and there will be more candles around. And then we can really start thinking about how to reinvent our fraternity and live like brothers and sisters all around the world. —*Ousmane Pame*

My spiritual practices. I go back to my roots, really looking at who I am and what I'm doing on this planet Earth. I imagine myself like a tree; when there's wind blowing it can very well topple you over, but if the roots are deep you would withstand the wind. And that root for me is my spiritual practice. —*Myah Payel Mitra*

My Christian beliefs support me in this journey. I don't think I would have done it without knowing that Jesus is there to support me in my line of work. Some of the things that happen I cannot explain, and no book or course I've attended can explain the transformation that I've witnessed. —*Alistair Maigurira*

My faith has been the strongest driving force in my life and in the work I do. I do it with gratitude and a deep sense of awe and passion for the people I'm working with, although I'm aware of the difficulties they're facing. My strength has come from my spiritual roots and my spiritual practices. —*Peter Guess*

I connect deeply to my intuition, that quiet centre of myself that is truly who I am and is connected to everything. I keep grounded by continuing to go back to that place and make decisions and move forward in my life based on what my intuition tells me to do, rather than what the outside world tells me to do. —*Julie Trager*

I trust in the greater plan. I've learned to listen to my intuition and calm my ego, and I know that everything happens for a reason. This gives me such a sense of peace and serenity and fearlessness, that I feel equipped to handle any of life's challenges with no limit to my level of audaciousness. —*Helen Strong*

Trusting the gravity that's holding your feet on the ground.
—*Claire Tonna*

An inner strength and belief in myself

The 'ness' is my strength to continue, knowing in my heart that I'm making an impact. And it doesn't matter if that impact is one person or a hundred people or a thousand people. Anyone who saves a life saves the whole universe. —*Dalia Feldheim*

My inner strength. I didn't always have it. Who I was when I was 20 is not who I am now. Who I am now is audacious and strong and bold and happy and content. It's about becoming Teflon in a way; things just roll off. And they have to roll off in order to maintain that strength. —*Andrea Heuston*

I believe in myself and I try to stay myself. It's important not to try to be someone else. The grounding is not dependent on other things; if you let go of everything and the columns start shaking, ultimately you're still there, you're still breathing. And as long as that's the case, you can still follow your dream. —*Felicia Specht*

It's a trust in myself, knowing that I can deal with anything. Living in nice and easy and comfortable surroundings doesn't really strengthen you. Like with muscles, if you don't train them, you don't develop them. So I feel trained in surviving, and this centres me. I trust myself. I know I can do this. —*Susanne Hillmer*

Pragmatism and trust. I look objectively at situations, assess what I can influence and what I cannot, then I focus on the former and let go of the latter. —*Maribel Ortega*

The fact that I love myself. I don't feel bad about saying that now but I could never say that before. When I was [pursuing my goal], I probably didn't love myself. What gave me the grounding to keep going then was the fact that I always knew I could overcome the next hurdle. But it was a fight to overcome those hurdles. So my advice to anyone else is to love themselves. —*Tish Joyce*

My grounding is my role as a mother and a wife. By understanding who I am, and who I am to others, I find a lot of stability and safety and security, even though everything else might be changing around me. —*Charlene Camilleri Duca*

The way I stay grounded is to check in with myself on a daily basis, monitoring my emotions and how I'm reacting to events. Being able to make conscious choices is the greatest asset we have. —*Gavin Scott*

This constant growing and feeling at ease and at peace, knowing that I'm living in alignment with my truth and doing the best I can. And practices that help with inner strength, confidence and connection with our higher selves, like yoga and wild swimming, things that bring us back to who we innately are. —*Jen Armstrong*

'Audaciousness' is body and mind; the two things have to be together. The 'ness' is the ground; it's our body, the earth element, the action. 'Audacious' is the courage – the willingness to receive yourself the way you are, and the courage to invest and reflect and know who you really are. —*Amaranatho*

A moral obligation

We've only got X number of breaths left on the planet, so what are we going to do with that? If we all chose to contribute to the betterment of humanity, that will happen. What are we doing here otherwise? How dare I not do something? —*Judy Boyle*

I feel a moral obligation. If I can help others and I can change somebody's life, for me not to do it would be like looking at somebody hanging off a cliff, having the ability to pick them up but then letting them hang there or fall. That moral obligation is the only thing that keeps me going. —*Timmy Douglas*

It's important to be part of something that's bigger than yourself. As a team member, if you don't do your job, not only do you let yourself down, but you let others down. And the biggest team game that we all play is this game of life. So be part of something that's bigger than yourself and I promise you, you'll have an exciting journey. —*Terry Tucker*

My joy in the learning journey

It's about enjoying the journey and not just seeing the end. So even if it's a stormy day, maybe the next day will be good. When I have moments where I'm down, then I appreciate the days that are good 300 times more. —*Cecilia Chiolerio*

It's a journey, not a destination, and the distance between two points is not a straight line. Just get there when you get there. As long as you're on the right track, you're making progress. If we look at the grand scheme of things, we do one small bit of the big goal at a time. —*Omolade Femi-Ajao*

My goal will never be achieved, but it's the journey. It's about finding my own self-care and balance and focusing on the small wins, finding the things that make me feel good and remind me of who I am and why I'm doing it.—*Debbie Levitt*

Seeing it as a journey and as a fun way of learning and growing and finding out what you're really capable of. Every single experience that you have, whatever it is, creates the person you are right now. It's a never-ending experience of learning and growing. —*Rebecca Allen*

My curiosity. I don't know where it comes from, but it's just this need to keep trying new things, to not stop and to explore what else can be done. So, to keep looking and learning and trying. —*Rika Cossey*

I value life and nature and learning, and that's what keeps me going. It's not easy being human, but if you live by your values and you get your energy from nature and you love learning, then you'll love life. And if you love life, then you won't let it get you. —*Philip Keay*

I feel that if I stop learning, I will not be alive anymore. —*Lynn Yap*

The support of friends and family

Making sure that you have the right people on the land with you. I always ask for support from the people I care about, listen to their opinion and make sure they see I'm doing the right thing, are proud of what I do and can help me out in any way. For me, that's the only way of going through these kinds of times. —*Cecilia Chiolerio*

One of the places I found my grounding was my husband because we're a team. I also have the inspiration of my mom, who is a very strong woman. I like having these two people around me – one to be strong and the other to keep a touch on what we have. —*Aurora Pérez-Vico*

My husband has encouraged me all the way through this. He's the one with the lifebelt and I wouldn't have done it without him, there's no question about that. He's the one I rely on for that firm foundation, when I spiral off a bit into the choppy waters. I know he's got my back, basically. He's the man! —*Denise Cowle*

My wife has been the solid ground that has permitted me to continue pursuing this goal. She has given me the peace of mind to understand that the actions we've taken, and the compromises we've been forced to make to enable the realisation of our goals, don't take away from the value we've created. —*Mark Matamisa*

I definitely have wobbles but what keeps me grounded is my family and my friends and nature. I feel when I've become disconnected from those things, I'm diminished. So making space for friendships, for family, for nature is what keeps me going – that centre of stability to be able to be more audacious. —*Farhana Yamin*

Solid grounding comes from having a great family. My mom, my dad, my sister, my brother are excellent. They're supportive. We're all wonderfully close. I love them all very much and if I needed their help, no matter what it was, I know that they're there. That's golden. I really appreciate it. —*Angela Papalia*

You're always going to stumble; we are not that solid ground. We are human; we stand on two feet and sometimes we get knocked down. And sometimes you've got to pick yourself back up. I've been very blessed with some people that look out for me and pick me up. They want to make sure I survive that storm. —*Colin O'Donohoe*

What grounded me in my cancer journey was my life purpose – my daughters. Everything I did was just focused on the need to heal physically, mentally, emotionally and spiritually, because I want to continue to be my daughters' mother and I want to be here and support them in their whole life. —*Jessa de la Morena*

It's always been my family and friends who support me, regardless of what I do, whatever crazy adventures or different experiments I want to try out. Their love and support for me has always helped me continue learning and to have the confidence to step out of my comfort zone. —*Lynn Yap*

The support I've had from everyone. If I didn't have people around me that believed in me and thought I was able to do it, I think it would have been a lot trickier for me to achieve my goals. —*Katie Taylor*

My family. My wife, in particular, is very supportive. And you need that sometimes when things are not going according to plan or things are taking longer than expected. So I would definitely say my family first. —*Nik Pandya*

It was the women that were behind me that gave me the confidence to carry on – my wife, my aunt and my mother. —*Kenneth Mackay*

Questions for the reader to consider

If you **have already done** something audacious, what gave you the solid grounding to continue with your audacious goal, despite everything life was throwing at you?

If you **would like to do** something audacious, think about what makes you want to get out of bed every morning and live each day. What gives you the solid grounding to continue despite everything life throws at you? Can you call on that grounding to make a start on your audacious path? Write down whatever comes up for you.

A Recipe for Leading an Audacious Life

We are each the creators of our own lives and, just like baking a cake, we can choose which ingredients to add and which method (or methods) to use to get the best results. Here is a suggested recipe, which we have put together from the wisdom shared by the 41 audacious guests we had the absolute pleasure of speaking (and, more importantly, listening) to. Feel free to modify it according to your personal tastes.

Ingredients

Your purpose for being
Your instinct (or gut feeling)
Utmost trust in a greater force
A curiosity and willingness to learn
The ability to observe what's around you
The ability to reframe and reformulate
Perseverance and grit
Acute self-awareness
Your authentic self
Lots of self-care

Method

1. Discover your purpose for being and what you are being called to do. Trust in your instinct and the greater force which is guiding all our lives.

2. Develop a curiosity and a willingness to learn. Observe what is happening around you and be aware of how you're perceiving it. Reframe your perception if need be.

3. Keep at what you're doing and don't give up. Cultivate a level of perseverance and grit to get you past any challenges you may encounter.

4. Become aware of who you are and how you react to situations. Always be authentic. Above all, take the utmost care of yourself.

5. Enjoy your audacious life. Let your light shine brightly in order to inspire others to also live their lives audaciously. After all, that's what it's all about!

Closing Thoughts

We set out writing this book with the purpose of collating the experiences and wisdom of 41 intrepidly bold and daring people into one volume. Our aims were threefold:

- To make sense of what we've learned from the utterly audacious people we interviewed in the last two years.

- To find common threads and patterns from what these people said, and to establish if there is indeed a blueprint or a mindset characteristic of audacious people.

- To offer tips and advice for others who wish to develop their audaciousness, set themselves bold goals, honour their genius and live their calling.

We feel that we've achieved what we set out to do and we hope you have enjoyed accompanying us on our journey of discovery. If you have been keeping a personal journal while reading this book, we'd suggest jotting down your immediate responses to the following questions:

1. What is your main takeaway from this book? What have you learned from the stories that these 41 audacious people have shared with us?

2. What other common threads or patterns emerged for you than the ones we identified? Is there indeed a blueprint for living an audacious life?

3. What tip or piece of advice did you find most helpful in developing your own audaciousness? What is your next step in your audacious journey?

What's next?

We feel our podcast project has taken on a mind of its own and that we were powerless to stop its evolution (or rather, we chose to step back and observe with eager curiosity where the journey was taking us). Bearing in mind that our ultimate goal was to enable a courageous community that honours their genius and lives their calling, then it seemed natural that the next step would be the publication of this book. This was followed by the website and finally the creation of the AudaciousNess Club.

Our vision for the future is to bring into being a group of people who will be inspired to act with the courage to create a positive impact in the world and thus provide inspiration for others to do the same. To this end, we intend to run regular themed events, either online or in person, to help people discover what may be hindering them from leading an audacious life and what steps they can take to get them started on that path.

If this sounds like something for you, then please check out the website at *https://audaciousness.club* and sign up to the mailing list to be kept up-to-date on all things audacious.

Thank you for engaging with the content of this book. We look forward to welcoming you to the club!

Helen & Maribel

Our Utterly Audacious
Podcast Guests

Maryam Mohiuddin Ahmed
(Ep. 19: Faith And Alignment)
Maryam grew up in Pakistan and has dedicated her life to social justice and human rights. She is the founder and director of Social Innovation Lab, an initiative that has helped 150 entrepreneurs start businesses, which have gone on to directly impact over 6 million people around the world.

Rebecca Allen
(Ep. 26: Create Your Own Outcomes)
Rebecca grew up in Hong Kong and now lives in Sydney with her husband and two children. In 2008, she gave up her advertising career to start her own coaching business, helping women execs build their personal brands and achieve career success.

Amaranatho
(Ep. 9: Our Best Role Model Is Nature)
Amaranatho was a Buddhist monk for 15 years and has spent long periods of time alone, in isolation and dealing with uncertainty. He now coaches executives, leaders and other coaches to improve their mindfulness and ability to self-reflect, so they can stay calm and connected in complex situations.

Jen Armstrong
(Ep. 37: A Voice For The Voiceless)

Jen is an English singer and songwriter who uses her musical talents to stand up for what she truly believes in. Jen writes songs that give a voice to those who are silenced and oppressed, whether human or animal, and released her debut album, *Freedom Warrior*, in the summer of 2022.

Vicky Arundel
(Ep. 7: Yoga Therapy)

Vicky founded a yoga therapy practice that offers one-to-one yoga specifically tailored to each individual's body, lifestyle and health needs. Her mission is to help people discover optimal wellbeing through the healing power of yoga.

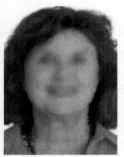

Judy Boyle
(Ep. 10: Fighting Human Trafficking)

Judy has been involved in anti-slavery campaigning for decades. Her award-winning non-profit organisation, *The NO Project*, targets youth awareness of modern slavery and human trafficking through film, music, art, dance, theatre, journalism, creative writing, education and social media.

Cecilia Chiolerio
(Ep. 4: Cool Co-Working Spaces)

Cecilia co-founded a company that provides low-cost, flexible co-working spaces in major European cities. By using cafés, bars and restaurants that are not usually open for business during the day, she offers professionals a quiet yet welcoming and collaborative place to do their work.

Anne Cholawo
(Ep. 22: Island On The Edge)
Anne took the bold decision to swap her hectic urban lifestyle in 1980s England for one of rural isolation and self-sufficiency on a tiny Scottish island, without mains electricity, shops or any other modern amenities.

Rika Cossey
(Ep. 16: Becoming Self-Sufficient)
Rika has spent her adult life travelling and living in countries all over the world. In 2018 she moved to rural Sweden with her husband and two young children, living in a tiny house before buying a farm. Rika and her family are now attempting to live as self-sufficiently and as close to nature as possible.

Denise Cowle
(Ep. 5: A Leap Into The Unknown)
After 25 years as a physiotherapist in the UK National Health Service, Denise made a bold career move when she decided to quit her stable job without knowing where she was going. She then found her passion and purpose in editing and proofreading.

Timmy Douglas
(Ep. 33: Alleviating World Poverty)
Timmy is a podcaster, coach and entrepreneur from Austin, Texas, who has set himself the audacious goal of alleviating world poverty.

Charlene Camilleri Duca
(Ep. 36: Adapting Your Dreams)
Charlene is a Clinical Psychologist and the Managing Director of two psychology clinics in Malta. In 2021/2022 she travelled around Europe for nine months with her husband and two-year-old son, living in rented accommodation for a week at a time and shifting her work online.

Dalia Feldheim
(Ep. 40: Dare To Lead Like A Girl)
As a marketing executive at Procter & Gamble, Dalia led some of the world's most iconic advertising campaigns. She now runs heart-centred leadership development programs with a mission to help organisations find purpose and joy at work.

Dr Omolade Femi-Ajao
(Ep. 8: Influencing Government Policy)
Omolade is a researcher and lecturer at the University of Manchester, focusing on improving the access of ethnic minority and immigrant women in high-income countries to existing health, social and community services.

Peter Guess
(Ep.28: Let's Talk About Race)
Peter and his business partner Alistair Maigurira (see below) run a diversity and inclusion consultancy in South Africa, called SALTAR (South Africa Let's Talk About Race). Their vision is to create a connection between people and, ultimately, a more inclusive world.

Andrea Heuston
(Ep. 1: Attitude And Abundance)
Andrea is an award-winning entrepreneur and founder and CEO of the creative agency Artitudes, where they create confident speakers. She also runs a podcast called *Lead Like a Woman*, which empowers women to empower others.

Susanne Hillmer
(Ep. 31: Professional Housesitting)
Self-employed since 2003, Susanne started to transform her business model in 2015 to enable her to work online from whichever location she happens to find herself in, either while living in her campervan or doing professional housesitting.

Tish Joyce
(Ep. 34: Running Across Europe)
Following a bold decision she made in 2017, Tish started an epic venture to run solo across five European countries, covering the equivalent of a marathon a day, with just a backpack, a tent and a pair of running shoes.

Philip Keay
(Ep. 30: The Accidental Emigrant)
Philip accidentally emigrated to Thailand in 1991, where he accidentally became a teacher. Having published his book, *Menu for a Spiritual Revolution*, in 2021, Philip now devotes his life to revolutionising education for the healing of humankind.

Debbie Levitt
(Ep. 13: Fixing The UX Industry)
Debbie's goal is to improve customer experience (CX) and user experience (UX) professions, as well as product and service experiences for customers. She runs her own consultancy and YouTube Channel and has recently published her first book.

Kenneth Mackay
(Ep. 41: The Road To Rhenigidale)
Kenneth campaigned tirelessly throughout the 1970s and 1980s to have a paved road built to his remote village on a Scottish island. After a long and arduous struggle, the road was finally opened in 1990 and the future of Kenneth's village was secured.

Alistair Maigurira
(Ep. 28: Let's Talk About Race)
Alistair and his business partner Peter Guess (see above) run a diversity and inclusion consultancy in South Africa, called SALTAR (South Africa Let's Talk About Race). Their vision is to create connection between people and, ultimately, a more inclusive world.

Mark Matamisa
(Ep. 14: Safe Drinking Water)
Mark is based in Cape Town, South Africa. After discovering in 2008 that not everyone in his homeland of Zimbabwe had access to clean drinking water, he and his friends set up an enterprise, *Project Oasis*, to provide safe, treated drinking water to a number of families in the country.

Myah Payel Mitra
(Ep. 11: Living Life By Design)
Myah is an award-winning Employee Engagement and Career Transition Coach recognized as one of the Top 5 Women Entrepreneurs working on mental health, leadership and well-being. She enables individuals, teams and organizations to get energized and live by design and not by default.

Jessa de la Morena
(Ep. 21: You Are The Hero)
After battling cancer twice and finding the positive support of people in similar situations lacking, Jessa started a community called *U Are the Hero*. Her goal is to provide a platform for inspirational stories which will empower people to take the reins of their own health and wellness and, ultimately, their lives.

Colin O'Donohoe
(Ep. 15: World Maestro)
Colin founded the Pangean Orchestra, an ensemble of performers and instruments from all over the world. Recognised as an outstanding composer, performer and arts advocate through awards, commissions, and grants, Colin's international impact has earned him the title of World Maestro.

Nahia Orduña
(Ep. 3: Digital Reinvention)
Nahia is an agile leader in disruption, a data and artificial intelligence (AI) evangelist, a future of work expert and a lifelong learner. Her book, *Your Digital Reinvention*, published in 2020, is a practical guide to helping people discover new job opportunities and find their place in the digital world.

Maribel Ortega
(Ep. 42: In Search Of Adventure)
In this episode, Maribel shares how she deals with life's highs and lows, how she comforts her inner critic during the low points, and the strategies she has developed for dealing with people who criticise her choices.

Dr Ousmane Pame
(Ep. 18: Reviving The Sahel)
Ousmane is the founder and director of a network of eco-villages in Senegal and Mauritania, in the Sahel. He is one of many people working to revive the now desertified region to the lush and abundant habitat it once was.

Nik Pandya
(Ep. 32: 21st Century Skills)
Nik is a primary and secondary level educator who, frustrated with the current state of the school system, is working to transform education and equip children with more relevant life skills for our modern times.

Angela Papalia
(Ep. 12: Remote Working From Mexico)
In 2020, after studying in Australia, then practising law for over ten years in Canada, Angela made the audacious decision to shift her work online and travel (mostly around Mexico), where she is enjoying a slower-paced and much more authentic life.

Mike Patterson
(Ep. 27: Question Everything)
Mike is a business consultant based in the United Arab Emirates who has so far helped over 50,000 people achieve their dreams. A keen researcher who has never believed in conforming, Mike has spent the last 20 years studying facts and figures in search of the truth.

Aurora Pérez-Vico
(Ep. 25: Alpha Vitamin Women)
Originally from Spain, Aurora lives with her husband and three young sons in Germany. She constantly strives to improve her skills and knowledge and she receives tremendous support and energy from her local network of 'Alpha Vitamin Women'.

Gavin Scott
(Ep. 38: Waking People Up)
Gavin is a motivational speaker and podcaster who provides leadership through self-demonstration and inspires people to question the programming and conditioning we have received, thus enabling us to make life decisions from an increased level of consciousness.

Felicia Specht
(Ep. 17: Challenging Societal Norms)
Following in her grandfather's footsteps, at the young age of 29 Felicia founded a company in the male-dominated architectural industry. She also established a network that provides support to around 250 young women working in the creative industries.

Helen Strong
(Ep. 43: Let God Set Your Goals)
In this episode, Helen talks about her encounter with God after being a non-believer for most of her life. She explains that letting ourselves be directed from a higher place means our goals will be much more audacious than what our tiny minds could ever come up with.

Jen Taylor
(Ep. 2: Homeschooling In A Campervan)
In the 2013/14 academic year, Jen and her husband Neil, sons Adam (15), Matt (13) and daughter Katie (9 – see below) travelled around Europe in a campervan, managing family life, education and a budget of €10 per person per day.

Katie Taylor
(Ep. 35: Natural Horsemanship)
Katie is the daughter of Jen (see above), who has set herself the audacious goal of becoming an expert in Natural Horsemanship. Due to a home-schooled upbringing, Katie has developed the skills, confidence and resourcefulness to achieve whatever she wants.

Claire Tonna
(Ep. 24: Trust The Nothing)
Claire is a Maltese singer/songwriter who uses the power of words and music to give 'strength and courage and a sense of belonging in a pretty much lonely world'. Through her audacious actions, she has evolved a highly philosophical view of life and death.

Julie Trager
(Ep. 29: Being A Fierce Life-Warrior)
Julie is a writer, a channel and a spiritual mentor based in California. After 15 years working in hospice and palliative care, which eventually led to burnout, Julie surrendered herself to God.

Terry Tucker
(Ep. 39: Faith, Family And Friends)
Terry is a motivational speaker based in Denver, Colorado, who has experienced a very varied life and career path. Since 2012, Terry has battled a rare form of cancer which led to his leg being amputated and now dedicates his life to helping people discover their uniqueness.

Farhana Yamin
(Ep. 6: The Power Of Communities)
Farhana is an environmental lawyer based in the UK. She is an active participant in her local community, bringing people together to develop ideas and projects tackling climate and ecological change.

Lynn Yap
(Ep. 20: Altruistic Capitalism)
Lynn grew up in Malaysia and moved to the UK at the age of 19 to study law. Her career has taken her from law to investment banking to launching a network supporting women and girls in work.

Index of Concepts

abundance 66

admiration 28, 114, 117, 118

advice 13, 15, 24, 33, 76, 90, 91, 98, 100, 117, 119, 135–149, 154, 162

alignment 12, 16, 24, 49, 62, 68, 99, 125, 126, 130, 134, 136, 155, 164

aspiration 118, 122, 123

attitude 12, 53, 80, 113, 115, 168

audaciousness, meaning of 11–12, 44, 150, 155, 163

authenticity 12, 24, 48, 49, 51, 66, 68, 98, 123, 128, 130, 133, 134, 160, 161, 171, 180

awareness 34, 37, 40, 51, 72, 78, 106, 111, 112, 119, 123, 124, 128, 129, 132, 148, 153, 160, 161, 158

balance 55, 88, 111, 130, 156, 180

behaviour 26, 37, 48, 53, 59, 63, 66, 67, 76, 93, 94, 97, 112, 114, 115, 126

beliefs 27, 45, 53, 54, 56, 58–62, 64, 67, 69, 70, 71, 75, 77, 78, 81, 85, 90, 92, 94, 96, 97, 99, 102, 117, 123, 125–129, 145, 151–154, 159, 165, 172, 173, 178

boundaries, setting 63, 64, 92, 133, 139, 140

calling, following your 10, 12, 13, 15, 22–24, 38, 43–52, 101, 161–163, 178, 180

challenges 9, 23, 31, 62, 65, 67, 73, 75, 77, 78, 81, 96, 101–113, 117, 131-133, 143, 148, 152, 153, 161

choices 13, 14, 27, 30, 31, 65, 84, 88–90, 94, 105, 127, 155, 171

comfort zone 9, 55, 66, 67, 133, 143, 147, 154, 159

community 10, 14–15, 33, 35, 40, 92, 93, 95, 96, 102, 107, 108, 111, 122, 126–128, 131, 138, 163, 167, 170, 174

conditioning 23, 45, 65, 83, 88, 93, 112, 132, 172

confidence 12, 27, 30, 33, 72, 84, 103, 112, 115, 119, 144, 155, 159, 168, 173

conforming 39, 47, 116, 130, 172

consciousness 48, 72, 81, 82, 112, 123, 127, 139, 155, 172

control 26, 28, 32, 38, 53, 56, 57–59, 70, 71, 78, 109, 133, 137

courage 10, 12, 15, 46, 54, 99, 155, 163, 173

creativity 9, 73, 74, 112, 118

criticism 31, 76, 79, 87, 90, 92, 93-98, 130, 171

curiosity 32, 33, 55, 82, 112, 156, 160, 161, 163

decisions 10, 11, 18, 21, 22, 23, 28, 29, 35, 38, 41, 43, 50, 55, 58, 59, 62, 63, 65, 69, 80–82, 84, 85, 88–91, 95, 103–105, 111, 112, 120, 127, 136–138, 144, 145, 153, 166, 168, 171, 172, 180

destiny 20, 38, 52, 57

discovery 10, 11, 20, 23, 29, 34–36, 42, 46–50, 53, 61, 64, 75, 76, 80, 95, 115, 121, 127, 129, 132, 133, 135, 142, 161–163, 165, 169, 170, 174, 178, 180

dreams 4, 21, 22, 26, 41, 42, 44, 48, 52, 54–57, 79, 81, 99, 105, 127, 154, 167, 172, 179

emotions 5, 8, 28, 35, 40, 45, 62, 66, 67, 69, 83, 91, 133, 139, 140, 155, 158, 180, 181 empowering 35, 46, 61, 99, 110, 128, 168, 170

environment 47, 49, 57, 69, 95, 97, 107, 112, 115, 119, 131, 132, 138, 174

expectations 15, 31, 33, 47, 55, 56, 59, 63, 75, 76, 78, 79, 89–91, 97, 107, 116, 130, 142, 159

experience 11, 15, 18, 23, 26–29, 33, 35, 39, 40, 44, 47, 49, 59, 64, 75, 80, 83, 84, 88, 91–93, 96, 113, 117–119, 125, 129, 130, 142, 149, 156, 162, 169, 174

failure 29, 36, 54–57, 67, 74, 75, 77–81, 86, 100, 113

faith 46, 53, 68, 69, 71, 90, 131, 151–153, 164, 174, 180

fear 4, 18, 23, 29, 33, 39, 64, 69, 73–75, 77–83, 85–87, 92, 96, 108, 125, 133, 134, 138, 153, 178, 179

feedback 4, 13, 33, 77–79, 87, 88, 90, 147

fulfilment 8, 27, 30, 94, 112, 115, 118, 125, 130, 178,

genius 5, 10, 13, 15, 73, 162, 163,

goals 10, 11, 13, 21, 24, 39, 46–48, 53–57, 60, 64, 66–68, 70, 71, 73, 77, 81, 83, 86, 92, 97, 101, 105, 109, 111, 113, 118, 123–127, 129, 132, 135, 141, 143–146, 148–150, 152, 154, 156–159, 162, 163, 166, 169, 170, 173, 178

grounding 11, 23, 31, 61, 90, 103, 130, 149–159

guilt 16, 25, 31, 64, 74, 83–86, 127

habits 49, 57, 93

harmony 23, 25, 132, 134, 180

honesty 5, 12, 31, 66, 69, 83, 134, 147

humanity 69, 110, 111, 126, 152, 155, 179

impostor syndrome 74–78, 86, 108

inner wisdom 122, 136, 178

inspiration 4, 15, 23, 30, 57, 67, 76, 91, 115, 117, 118, 122, 123, 132, 146, 157, 163, 170

intention 88, 92, 98, 99, 114

intuition 17, 23, 24, 41, 74, 83, 91, 130, 153

journey 13, 15, 23, 32, 48, 59, 62, 83, 94, 98, 101, 102, 106, 127, 131, 144, 146, 147, 149, 152, 156, 158, 162, 163, 178

joy 12, 21, 35, 51, 69, 97, 126, 128, 156, 167, 179

judgement 33, 94, 123

knowledge 14, 18, 23, 60, 61, 76, 82, 102, 108, 118, 119, 136, 152, 172

learning 13, 17, 29, 55, 59, 61, 63, 76, 82, 102–112, 135, 141, 144, 145, 156, 157, 159

limitations 23, 64, 70, 73, 81, 116, 127, 153

mentors 29, 69, 84, 115, 119–122, 127, 130, 174, 178

mindset 13, 28, 29, 42, 52–71, 92, 101, 121, 138, 147, 162, 179, 181

motivation 4, 35, 39, 48, 94, 114, 122, 125, 172, 174

obligation (moral) 129, 155

pain points 20, 125, 129, 149

passion 17, 26, 45, 46, 48–51, 60, 66, 112, 132, 144, 151, 153, 166

perception 37, 75, 84, 96, 99, 124, 161

perseverance 66, 92, 144, 145, 160, 161

perspective 12, 28, 57, 92, 93, 99, 116, 135

plans 9, 17, 23, 51, 53, 54, 56, 57, 59, 71, 78–80, 83, 103, 104, 139, 140, 145, 146, 153, 159, 178, 180

potential 9, 21, 32, 45, 49, 55, 61, 70, 94, 97, 114, 123, 128, 130, 181

power 27, 32, 45, 48, 49, 60, 78, 81, 165, 173, 174, 178, 180

preparation 31, 70, 77, 90, 105, 113, 132, 144, 148

procrastination 78, 144, 147

programming (cultural) 62, 74, 93, 112, 172, 179

purpose 10, 14, 18, 28, 35, 39, 46, 48, 52, 54, 61, 66, 97, 119, 125, 126, 130, 134, 135, 143, 151, 158, 160–162, 166, 167, 179

reactions 31, 48, 63, 65, 79, 84, 87–90, 93, 95, 100, 105, 117, 133, 155, 161

re-framing 61, 78, 84, 160, 161, 179

responsibility 31, 56, 62, 63–65, 80, 84, 85, 91, 92, 97

role model 10, 16, 30, 99, 114–123, 145, 164

scarcity 65, 66

self-awareness (see awareness)

self-care 135, 139–141, 156, 160, 161

self-confidence (see confidence)

self-control 59, 133

self-doubt 11, 60, 70, 73, 74, 76, 85, 90, 91, 94, 108, 119, 178

self-esteem 25, 30, 31, 74

selfishness 26, 65, 141

selflessness 96, 141

service (being of) 60, 69, 96, 104, 107, 109, 125–127, 129

shame 27, 84, 127

society 12, 16, 23, 26, 36, 45, 47, 54, 66, 69, 74, 94, 95, 106, 109, 112, 116, 126, 128, 130, 132, 172, 180

solutions 26, 104–106, 108, 110, 131, 133, 178

strength 45–47, 49, 62, 65, 68, 98, 99, 108, 117, 137, 149, 153–155, 157, 173

stress 37, 41, 70, 140–142, 145

success 38, 62, 67, 73–77, 80, 81, 86, 111, 118, 139, 164, 179, 181

talents 8, 45, 47, 61, 74, 94, 100, 112, 120, 165, 178

thoughts 41, 67, 70, 79, 90, 92

transformation 17, 35, 51, 79, 92, 93, 127, 171

trauma 110

trust 17, 23, 24, 28, 31, 32, 51, 53, 58, 62, 63, 68, 69, 71, 76, 85, 90, 91, 106, 107, 120, 153, 154, 160, 161, 173, 180

truth 31, 60, 65, 66, 68, 69, 75, 84, 85, 98, 99, 123, 134, 145, 155, 172

ubuntu 68, 69, 125

uniqueness 45, 61, 100, 174, 178

values 24, 62, 68, 96, 124–134, 137, 140, 152, 157

vision 28, 41, 54, 57, 82, 90, 96, 109, 123, 128, 151, 163, 167, 169

voice 23, 25, 27, 32, 40, 46, 51, 69, 72–74, 79, 84, 85, 98, 99, 165

wisdom 11, 14, 23, 160, 162,

Further Reading

We've all got our own unique paths to follow, and there's no one right way to go about things. That's why we wanted to share a few of our favourite books with you. These books have helped us navigate the path of our own individual audacious journeys, and we hope they can help guide others like you in your own bold and daring pursuits.

Self-Coaching

Playing Big by Tara Mohr
An easy-to-read and practical book that presents a solution to recognising and owning our talent and living a more fulfilling life. Tara Mohr walks us through discovering barriers such as the inner critic and tuning into our wisdom, which she calls the inner mentor. This comprehensive guide helps us work through fear, communicate with power, find our calling and embrace ease.

Be Your Own Life Coach by Fiona Harrold
Life coach Fiona Harrold makes a commitment in this book to help the reader move beyond the doubts and fears that are holding them back, to believe in themselves and to develop a plan of action for reaching their goals and desires in order to change their lives for the better. For anyone wishing to achieve big, hairy, audacious goals, this book shows you how.

Dealing with the Inner Critic

Feel the Fear and Do It Anyway by Susan Jeffers
A great resource for handling the inner critic. In this book Susan Jeffers explains that by changing our mindset we can achieve whatever we want, despite feeling fear. Topics covered include reframing 'mistakes', letting go of negative programming, saying yes to opportunities, finding purpose and meaning in our lives and turning dreams into reality.

Feeding Your Demons by Tsultrim Allione
In this partly autobiographical book – and inspired by a Buddhist spiritual practice called Chod, which means 'to cut through' – Tsultrim Allione explains her five-step method to resolving inner conflicts. A demon is anything that obstructs the achievement of freedom (fears, obsessions, addictions). Allione encourages us to befriend what we want to avoid: to nurture instead of battle our inner and outer enemies.

Spiritual Guidance

The Seven Spiritual Laws of Success by Deepak Chopra
This little handbook briefly covers some of the natural laws of the universe and how to apply them to our own lives in order to find our purpose and be of service to humanity. Deepak Chopra explains how we can use these universal laws to fulfil our dreams and desires with the least effort, develop a mindset of abundance and live a joyful and healthy life.

The Surrender Experiment by Michael A Singer
Michael A Singer truly followed his calling when he decided to surrender himself completely to what life had in store for him, laying his own personal plans aside and trusting in whatever the universe was sending his way. This is a fascinating account of a life spent in utmost faith in, and surrender to, a higher power way more intelligent than any mere human can ever be.

Connecting with our Authentic Selves

Rise Sister Rise by Rebecca Campbell
Not just for women, this book is a clarion call for the restoration of the masculine–feminine balance after millennia of living in a far too linear and hierarchical society. It is an invitation for the intuitive, powerful and fierce feminine force that exists within each of us to rise, so that we can all step up and bring our relationship with our planet back into balance and harmony.

It's Not Always Depression by Hilary Jacobs Hendel
An unfortunate title for quite a useful book that shows us how to listen to our bodies, discover our core emotions and connect with our authentic self. Hilary Jacobs Hendel introduces 'the Change Triangle' as a tool to understand our emotions and detect the defence mechanisms we use to avoid them, plus other techniques to help us spend more time in the open-hearted state of the authentic self.

Positive Communication and Mindset

Positive Intelligence by Shirzad Chamine

Backed by scientific research, Shirzad Chamine presents in this book the concept of the Positive Intelligence Quotient (PQ), arguing that it is more important for success than IQ (Intelligence Quotient) or EQ (Emotional Intelligence Quotient), and that it is a skill we can train. Having a positive mindset determines the likelihood of reaching our potential.

Drop the Pink Elephant by Bill McFarlan

A fun-to-read book by an expert in communication and public speaking, Bill McFarlan's message is to focus on the positive and talk about what we want our listeners to think about. This book is packed with practical advice for communicating effectively, answering any type of difficult question and building relationships.

Ingram Content Group UK Ltd.
Milton Keynes UK
UKHW040636220523
422126UK00001B/6

9 781739 371104